Martin Luther King Jr.
on Creative Living

D1564057

Martin Luther King Jr.
on Creative Living

MICHAEL G. LONG

CHALICE
PRESS

ST. LOUIS, MISSOURI

Cover photo: © DPA/Landov
Cover design: Lynne Condellone
Interior design: Elizabeth Wright
Art direction: Elizabeth Wright

This book is printed on acid-free, recycled paper.

Visit Chalice Press on the World Wide Web at
www.chalicepress.com

10 9 8 7 6 5 4 3 2 1   04 05 06 07 08 09

Library of Congress Cataloging–in–Publication Data

Long, Michael G.
Martin Luther King Jr. on creative living / Michael G. Long.
   p. cm.
ISBN 0-8272-0496-5 (pbk. : alk. paper)
1. Christian life—Meditations. 2. King, Martin Luther, Jr., 1929-1968. I. Title.
BV4501.3.L655 2004
248.4—dc22

2004005329

Printed in the United States of America

Table of Contents

Acknowledgments

"You conquer self-centeredness," Martin Luther King Jr. preached, "by coming to the point of seeing that you are where you are today because somebody helped you to get there."[1] I am not sure if it would ever be possible for me to conquer the seductive power of self-centeredness, but I am certain that King has helped me to understand that I am where I am today because countless "somebodies" have helped me along the way. Indeed, I am greatly indebted to King, a friend I have never hugged, a fellow traveler I have never walked with, and a mentor I have never thanked, for inviting me to see and embrace "the beloved community" that exists far beyond my computer screen.

With King's words in my heart, I am more than aware that this book is the product of not only my work, but also the contributions of numerous friends, family members, and colleagues. And I am deeply grateful for that community especially during this bleak midwinter season, when death and loss have sought to silence creativity in my life.

I am especially grateful to Sharon Herr, a cherished friend, for her extraordinary work in proofreading my manuscript, and more importantly, for her constant support. Jane McAvoy, editorial director at Chalice Press, deserves my gratitude for her expert eye and steady hand in guiding the complicated process of publication. I thank Christine Bucher, Chair of the Department of Religious Studies at Elizabethtown College, for her exceptional leadership of the department during the writing stages. And how could I not express my thanks to Carol Morris for reminding me time and again that creative living is a matter of the heart.

I reserve my deepest gratitude for Karin and Jackson Long especially, for allowing me to wrestle, sometimes exhaustingly, with

---

[1]Martin Luther King Jr., "Conquering Self-Centeredness," *Symbols of the Movement: January 1957–December 1958*, vol. 4 of *The Papers of Martin Luther King, Jr.*, ed. Clayborne Carson et al. (Berkeley: University of California Press, 1992), 239.

the meaning of creative living in terms of my daily life. With the completion of these acknowledgments, Jack and I can go to the station and hold hands while we watch the evening train begin its journey to Philadelphia. For me, life is simply beautiful in those moments when he and I pause to enjoy the present moment, and then to imagine where life might take us. In the deepest recesses of my heart, I thank him and Karin for granting me the joy of being a father. As I write this, my greatest hope is that I will somehow help Jack understand the importance of living a life that is full of passion and creativity—a life for which he, too, will be grateful.

Michael Long
Winter 2004

The Heart of Creative Living

"Is your heart right?"[1] This is the searching question that the Reverend Doctor Martin Luther King Jr. posed to his congregation at Ebenezer Baptist Church in Atlanta just one month before his tragic assassination in 1968. It was a year when the United States, with urban riots at home and a determined opponent in Vietnam, seemed far from peaceful, let alone righteous. Struggling with his own patterns of behavior, personal and social, King called upon his church members to get on "the right road" of life—not to be concerned about the separate mistakes they had made along the way, but to ensure that the whole of their life steered in the right direction.[2] It was easy, at least for those who knew him well, to imagine that King, a relentless critic of his own moral failings, was also preaching to himself.

It was a depressing period for him. King's dream had shattered so many times that by 1968 his heart seemed broken, his body worn

---

[1]Martin Luther King Jr., "Unfulfilled Dreams," in *A Knock at Midnight: Inspiration from the Great Sermons of Reverend Martin Luther King, Jr.*, ed. Clayborne Carson and Peter Holloran (New York: Warner Books, 1998), 198. I will return to this sermonic theme in the last chapter.

[2]Ibid., 197.

1

2 *Martin Luther King Jr. on Creative Living*

down, and his eyes on the brink of tears. Ever aware of others, he also realized that it was not only his dream that had shattered through the years; his people's dreams were crushed too—the people who sat before him that Sunday, family members and friends, hoping and waiting to receive the word of God.

King did not disappoint. "In times like these," he preached, "you need an anchor." The use of so many different metaphors—anchor, road, heart—did not matter to his friends, because they knew exactly where their preacher was going. In the rich call-and-response tradition of American black churches, they encouraged him to "keep on keeping on" toward the God who anchored their wandering hearts. "Yes," they shouted. "Glory to God!"[3]

King needed his Ebenezer friends in such tough times. He needed their encouragement, their support, and all the love he had felt from them ever since the very first days of his life, when Daddy King, a man of imposing presence, physical and spiritual, had stood in the pulpit the younger King now occupied. And his Ebenezer friends needed him too—his visionary leadership, his big appetite for their church dinners, his special concern for their family members. Clearly, King loved the Ebenezer members as much as they loved him, and he loved them so much he wanted to see them thrive in the life that disappointed them so deeply—not just to *survive* the tough times but to *flourish* in spite of them.

King was deeply aware that shattered dreams could easily lead his people, including those beyond Ebenezer, to become full of despair—the type of despair he saw all too clearly in the overflowing tears of mothers and fathers whose children had died in bombings carried out by vicious racists, in the slumped shoulders of black workers who could not earn a livable wage to feed and clothe their families, and in the wide-eyed stares of little black boys and girls who wondered why they could not swim in the beautiful pool where the white boys and girls had so much fun. King also feared that such despair would eventually become destructive, that it would break his people's spirits and bodies, and that it would erupt in violent events that could leave them, like Denmark Vesey and Nat Turner, dead for naught.

---

[3]Ibid., 199.

With the possibility of their senseless destruction in mind, and with abiding love for them in his heart, King implored his followers, even when he was at the lowest points of his own life, like in 1968, to practice what he called "creative living," the type of lifestyle that would put people "on the right road." He did not have a developed theory of creative living (after all, he was a preacher, not an armchair theorist), but throughout his life he had sketched separate pieces of what he meant by living creatively in a world of destruction. This book, a basic primer, is an attempt to bring together those scattered pieces and present them as a whole.

The book begins with King's desperate clinging to the Anchor— his unwavering belief that the one and only starting point of creative living is the God of love and justice as revealed in Jesus of Nazareth. King preached time and again that only God can pull us out of despair and set us on the right road to creative living—a life reflective of the love and justice that are an integral part of the character of God. If our hearts are not right, King preached, it is because we have not opened them to the God who can make a way out of no way, transforming hate into love, injustice into justice, and destructiveness into creativity.

The second chapter then describes King's understanding of creative living in the time of our lives—the past, present, and future. Unlike Christians who see earthly time as merely a burden to be suffered, a cross to be taken up and carried, King envisioned time as both a burden and a gift—a burden because it is marked by the presence of so much human sin, and a gift because it is the wondrous occasion to join God in creating "the beloved community" where justice and love will reign. Just so, King believed that creative living means keeping on keeping on, that is, rejecting part of the past, present, and future, but also affirming part of each as a key resource for discerning and acting on the will of God in human history.

Especially wary of people who get bogged down in the past, or fly off to heaven without concern for earthly life, King stressed that creative living means focusing on the here and now. Creative living in the present moment—discerning the presence of God, right here and right now, and mirroring the divine character in our everyday lives—has a variety of dimensions in King's thought, and this book will seek to unpack only the major ones. The third chapter will describe King's belief that creative living means a life of action—acting for the beloved community by eliminating structural oppression, forming moral character in the ways of Jesus, and creating social structures that reflect the love and justice of God. Moving beyond the theme of action, the fourth chapter will observe that King understood creative living to be a matter of not just doing but also being—retreating to the mountain, far from the pressing crowds, so that we can have time to reflect, pray, spend time with our family and friends, and thereby regain the energy we need for returning to a life of action in the valley. And the fifth chapter will highlight his belief that we can do none of this, either act or retreat creatively, unless we conquer the fear of our approaching death. King clearly believed that our ability to live creatively depends upon our willingness to hold a double attitude toward death, saying no to the pain of death and yes to the glorious fulfillment of dreams that God offers in death.

So are our hearts right? King believed that if our hearts are not right, it is because we are not making a sustained effort to depend on the Anchor and live creatively in response to the divine will that grounds us in groundless times. In fact, for King, sinful living was nothing less than quiet resignation to the destructive forces of life. King conceded, especially during difficult times, that the destructive forces may shatter lives for years to come, even countless years, but he found that to be no reason for us to roll over in despair and just die. What matters most, according to King, is that we try, with all of our power, to hold onto the Anchor through it all, trusting that God will always be with us, even in death; to dream of the beloved community that God intends not just for privileged whites but especially for "the least of these," those on the margins of society; to make the dream come alive in our personal character and the social structures of our communities; and to take the mountain time we need for refueling so that we can work even harder in the valley. What matters most in life is that we make an effort, the best effort possible, to live creatively. And if we do make that effort, King preached, we can and should rest assured—our heart will be right, we will be on the right road, and that will be good enough for God.

King's vision of creative living, highlighted here and detailed in the following pages, is a stellar example of works within the emerging field of practical theology and ethics. As you turn the pages, you will quickly note that the substance of this book is not abstruse academic theology, the type King studied while a graduate student at Boston University, but profoundly practical advice for everyday living. Indeed, I have sought to glean significant portions of his vision for creative living from a popular column he wrote for *Ebony*, "Advice for Living," which addressed everything from the color of Jesus' skin to the problems of rock-and-roll.

Because this book addresses King's practical theology and ethics, and because I intend for the book to be merely a basic primer, I have also sought to present the notion of creative living in an easily accessible way, giving heavy emphasis within the text to King's words rather than to my academic interpretation of them. If you would like to pursue the academic issues surrounding King's thought, including some of the key issues in contemporary King studies, I refer you to the book's footnotes, especially those in the first two chapters. The footnotes throughout the book address some of the more significant issues within King studies and, perhaps more importantly, list secondary literature that you might find helpful for pursuing King's thought in greater detail than I can even hope to offer in this primer.

Finally, a direct personal word about the subject of this book, as well as his audience, is in order. Recent years have proven difficult for the legacy of Martin Luther King Jr. Heavily documented studies of King's practice of plagiarism, in addition to loosely documented, indeed sensational, reports of his alleged womanizing, have saturated much of the recent mass media coverage of his life. In offering this brief study, I seek not to ignore or dismiss these charges and allegations, but rather to suggest that King's legacy, just like his moral character, can never be reduced to such matters as plagiarism and intimate behavior. The whole King is greater, far greater, than the man who borrowed words without attribution or who expressed interest in women other than his wife. In my estimation, the whole King includes not only those actions, real or imagined, but also his willingness to suffer for the God-given dignity of his brothers and sisters, his courage to stand against a government that sought to degrade him, his abiding love for his family and friends, his deep faith in the Anchor—and, of course, his compelling vision of creative living. Like each of us, the whole King is both sinner and saint.

Beyond character issues, I suggest that even if King had not acted on his vision at all times and in all places, the substance of his vision of creative living, in and of itself, has tremendous power to change lives, including ours. And this, at last, is the reason behind my decision to write this book. Although my own theological inclinations diverge significantly from King's Christian theism, I believe that his vision of creative living has the potential to transform our lives.

It is important to note here that King presented most of the following advice to his own people—African Americans in need of liberation from oppressive white structures. As you read the pages that follow, I hope you will remember that King's vision of creative living is, at many points, specifically targeted to the needs and desires of African Americans in the 1950s and '60s. In addition, you will see that King's language, typical of its patriarchal context, is exclusivist at points. I have chosen to preserve King's language, partly because of my belief that historical records should not seek to erase the sexism that pervaded even the civil rights movement.

But I also hope you will note that the general dimensions of his advice for creative living are not only deeply Christian but also profoundly humane. Holding to this view, I claim that significant parts of King's vision of creative living are useful for not only his own people but also the wider Christian community and the world beyond—for me, for you, and for all who are privileged to experience the vision and begin the slow process of transforming our lives from destructiveness to creativity.

CHAPTER ONE

Never Alone
Creative Living with God

"We were made for God," King preached in 1967, "and we will be restless until we find rest in him."[1] According to King, it is simply impossible for us to practice creative living without the comforting and challenging presence of God in our life together. God is the only one, the only personality, who can pull us out of a life of restlessness, even despair, and empower us to live as the creative individuals (and community) God has created us to be. Moreover, King believed that we can live creatively only when we begin to discern and follow the moral laws of God etched on our hearts— the principles of love and justice that are part of the very character

---

[1]Martin Luther King Jr., "The Three Dimensions of a Complete Life," *A Knock at Midnight: Inspiration from the Great Sermons of Reverend Martin Luther King, Jr.,* ed. Clayborne Carson and Peter Holloran (New York: Warner Books, 1998), 135. Behind King's words here are Augustine's early reflections on the restfulness found in God: "…you have made us for yourself, and our heart is restless until it rests in you, " Saint Augustine, *Confessions,* trans. Henry Chadwick (Oxford: Oxford University Press, 1992), 3. In addition, Keith Miller, *Voice of Deliverance: The Language of Martin Luther King, Jr., and Its Sources* (New York: The Free Press, 1992), 75–76, has noted that King borrowed heavily for this sermon from Phillips Brooks's sermon

of God. This means that nothing less than the character of God provides us with the substantive guidance we need for creative living. King believed that we can receive this guidance because God is not far removed from our everyday life, somewhere in the distant heavens, rarely to be disturbed, but is in history, right here and right now, struggling for love and justice, revealing the divine character, and ever ready to become our "cosmic companion." And so creative living—God-centered living—seeks not to escape from this world but to be embedded in it deeply, joining God in the creative effort to transform the world into "the beloved community," a time and place full of love and justice.[2]

---

titled "The Symmetry of Life," *Selected Sermons*, ed. William Scarlett (New York: Dutton, 1950), 195–206. Miller's excellent study addresses the controversial issue of King's plagiarism. Though King scholars debate the reasons for, as well as the extent and moral significance of, his plagiarism, they agree that King frequently used the works of others without attribution when writing his own sermons, essays, and books—so much so that, had his professors detected the plagiarism in his academic work, King most likely would not have received some of the degrees he earned. For a response to Miller on this topic, see Richard Lischer, *The Preacher King: Martin Luther King, Jr., and the Word That Moved America* (New York: Oxford University Press, 1995). More generally, see the *Journal of American History* 78, no.1 (June 1991) and the outstanding articles it devotes to King's plagiarism, including David Thelen, "Becoming Martin Luther King, Jr.: An Introduction," 11–22; "Conversation between S. Paul Schilling and Paul Thelen," 63–80; David Levering Lewis, "Failing to Know Martin Luther King, Jr.," 81–85; David Garrow, "King's Plagiarism: Imitation, Insecurity, and Transformation," 86–92; Clayborne Carson, with Peter Holloran, Ralph E. Luker, and Penny Russell, "Martin Luther King, Jr., as Scholar: A Reexamination of His Theological Writings," 93–105; Jim Higham, "Habits of the Cloth and Standards of the Academy," 106–10; Bernice Johnson Reagon, "'Nobody Knows the Trouble I See'; or, 'By and By I'm Gonna Lay Down My Heavy Load,'" 111–19; and Keith Miller, "Martin Luther King, Jr., and the Black Folk Pulpit," 120–23.

[2] I agree with Robert Michael Franklin, who writes: "King's entire ethical system is a species of theological ethics," in "An Ethic of Hope: The Moral Thought of Martin Luther King, Jr.," *Union Seminary Quarterly Review* 40 (January 1986): 43. In this first chapter I suggest that it is impossible to understand King's notion of creative living without tending to his doctrine of God. Indeed, the intent of this chapter is not to focus on the *practices* of creative living, as the following chapters will do, but on the doctrine of God that underlies King's vision of creative living. In addition, I also suggest throughout the book that it is impossible to grasp King's notion of creative living without unpacking his theological understanding of human nature, history, and the end times. Just so, King's thought on creative living is a species of his theological ethics.

No, Never Alone

"He promised never to leave me, never to leave me alone. No, never alone. No, never alone."[3] The comforting words of "Never Alone," one of King's favorite hymns, helped him witness time and again to his deep trust in the immediate, unfailing, and empowering presence of God in his life—a presence that King found not just helpful but also essential for creative living.[4]

King's personal testimony, which he offered throughout his life, grew out of a frightening moment of despair on a January night in 1956. It had been a long day of dealing with the never-ending demands of the famous bus boycott in Montgomery, and the end of this particularly stressful day stretched on, almost unbearably, when the phone rang just as King was beginning to doze in the comfort of his bed.

On the other end was a voice of rage: "Listen, nigger, we've taken all we want from you; before next week you'll be sorry you ever came to Montgomery." It was not a new message—King had

---

[3]Martin Luther King Jr., "Unfulfilled Dreams," *Knock*, 199. For more on the sources behind King's reflection on his kitchen epiphany, see Miller, *Voice of Deliverance*, 138–40.

[4]King's trust in the immediate, unfailing, and empowering presence of God remained constant throughout his lifetime. The question of constancy and evolution is important for fully understanding King's theology, especially his doctrine of God. Because this is a primer, I will not address all the fine nuances of King's thought—for example, the different characteristics of God that King emphasized at different points in his life. Still, even if I were to note the nuances, I would maintain that Carson is right to suggest that there is a general consistency in King's "basic religious and political convictions," including, I argue, those expressed in his doctrine of God. See Clayborne Carson, "Martin Luther King, Jr., and the African-American Social Gospel," in *African-American Religion: Interpretive Essays in History and Culture*, ed. Timothy Fulop and Albert Raboteau (New York: Routledge, 1997), 349. See also Thomas Mikelson's argument that there is significant continuity in King's doctrine of God—"Cosmic Companionship: The Place of God in the Moral Reasoning of Martin Luther King, Jr.," *Journal of Religious Ethics* 18 (Fall 1990): 1–14. More particularly, Mikelson argues that, as King's social thought became more radical in the last three years of his life, his doctrine of God remained essentially the same as before. For more on the radical theology of King in general, see Michael Eric Dyson, *I May Not Get There With You: The True Martin Luther King, Jr.* (New York: The Free Press, 2000); and Luther Ivory, *Toward a Theology of Radical Involvement: The Theological Legacy of Martin Luther King, Jr.* (Nashville: Abingdon Press 1997). A concise look at King's theology in relation to other theologies is Noel Leo Erskine, *King Among the Theologians* (Cleveland: The Pilgrim Press, 1994).

heard similar death threats so many times before—but on this troublesome night his soul had finally reached its "saturation point."

Unable to sleep, a frustrated and fearful King went to the kitchen to make a cup of coffee and think of ways to pull out of his leadership position.[5] He thought of his newborn daughter Yoki, his supportive wife Coretta, and the possibility of their deaths. "And I got to the point," King testified, "that I couldn't take it any longer, I was weak."

In times past, he had called upon Daddy and Mama King for comfort, strength, and encouragement, but this time he knew he needed a much greater power, "that power that can make a way out of no way," and so he bowed over the kitchen table and poured out all his fears, all his frustrations, and all his concerns. "I'm at the end of my powers," he prayed. "I have nothing left."[6]

---

[5]King was not always the fearless, strong, and certain leader that many present him as being. The literature on King and leadership is fascinating. Some authors (most notably, Donald T. Philips, *Martin Luther King, Jr., on Leadership: Inspiration & Wisdom for Challenging Times* [New York: Warner Books, 1998]) see King's overall leadership skills as exemplary. Others depict King as a great leader only in terms of the inspiration he offered to his followers. Peter J. Ling, for example, criticizes King's leadership in tactical matters. "King," Ling writes, "had never been a master strategist. Others had launched the Montgomery Bus Boycott, the Birmingham and Selma movement, and some of his young lieutenants, notably former sit-in student James Bevel, were more adept tactically." See "Martin Luther King's Half-forgotten Dream," *History Today* 48, no. 4 (April 1998): 19. Ling's criticism is not new. Nearly forty years ago, for example, August Meier wrote that King was "an ineffective administrator," in "On the Role of Martin Luther King," *New Politics* 4 (Winter 1965): 56. Ling attacks not only King's tactical skills, however; he also accuses King of *hubris*, a destructive pride of seeing himself as the only one who could lead his people nonviolently: "Martin Luther King's Half-forgotten Dream," 21. Hoping to move away from "what might be termed 'King-centric' studies," Ling continues his sharp criticism of King in *Martin Luther King, Jr.* (New York: Routledge, 2002), 2. "Without the activities of the movement," Ling writes, "most of which he did not control or orchestrate, Martin Luther King might well have been no more than just another black Baptist preacher who spoke well." Though he does not write as pointedly as Ling does, Clayborne Carson also wants to reduce King "to human scale" and note the significance of the many grassroots movements that were just as important as King's leadership in creating the conditions required for the advance of civil rights. See Clayborne Carson, "Martin Luther King, Jr.: Charismatic Leadership in a Mass Struggle, *Journal of American History* 74, no. 2 (September 1987): 453. This particular issue of *JAH* is devoted to a discussion of King as leader. Other articles on leadership in this issue include David Garrow, "Martin Luther King, Jr., and the Spirit of Leadership," 438–47; and Nathan Irvin Huggins, "Martin Luther King, Jr.: Charisma and Leadership," 477–81.

[6]Martin Luther King Jr., *The Autobiography of Martin Luther King, Jr.*, ed. Clayborne Carson (New York: Warner Books, 1998), 77.

But something happened at that kitchen table. With the final sigh of despair pouring out of him, and with nothing but nothing to grasp, King began to sense, ever so quietly, the inner power he desperately needed. "It seemed as though I could hear the quiet assurance of an inner voice saying, 'Martin Luther, stand up for righteousness. Stand up for justice. Stand up for truth. And lo, I will be with you. Even until the end of the world.'"[7] The voice was unmistakable to King in the quiet of the night—he understood it to be the comforting and challenging voice of the Spirit of Jesus. "But I heard the voice of Jesus," King testified, "saying still to fight on."[8]

The personal effect of hearing that voice was life-changing. "At that moment," King remarked, "I experienced the presence of the Divine as I had never experienced him before. Almost at once my fears began to go. My uncertainty disappeared. I was ready to face anything."[9] So rather than giving up his leadership of the budding movement, King became divinely assured of the righteousness of standing up and fighting on—and of the promise that, no matter what befell him, the Spirit of Jesus would always be with him, even until the end of the world, empowering him to do what is right. No, King would never be alone in his creative efforts to make a brighter day for his people—no, never alone.[10]

God Is Everywhere

King was a black Baptist preacher to the core of his being. His theology was first formed in the black church, especially under the preaching of Daddy King, and then in the social gospel tradition

---

[7]Ibid., 77–78.

[8]King, "Unfulfilled Dreams," *Knock,* 199.

[9]King, *Autobiography*, 78.

[10]For more important biographical stories in King's life, see Taylor Branch, *Parting the Waters: America in the King Years, 1954–63* (New York: Simon & Schuster, 1988); Branch, *Pillar of Fire: America in the King Years, 1963–65* (New York: Simon & Schuster, 1998); James Colaiaco, *Martin Luther King, Jr.: Apostle of Militant Nonviolence* (New York: St. Martin's Press, 1988); Adam Fairclough, *Martin Luther King, Jr.* (Athens: University of Georgia Press, 1990); Marshall Frady, *Martin Luther King, Jr.* (New York: Penguin, 2002); David J. Garrow, *Bearing the Cross: Martin Luther King, Jr., and the Southern Christian Leadership Conference* (New York: Vintage Books, 1986); David Levering Lewis, *King: A Critical Biography* (New York: Praeger, 1970); Ling, *Martin Luther King, Jr.*; and Stephen B. Oates, *Let the Trumpet Sound: The Life of Martin Luther King, Jr.* (New York: Harper & Row, 1982).

adopted by liberal Black scholars, including Benjamin Mays, president of Morehouse College, where King had enrolled at the age of fifteen. In addition, King's best preaching, usually done in front of black audiences, embodied the black church in substance and style. Indeed, true to the conclusion of many black church services, King often sought to convert those who heard him.[11] King thus wanted his followers, indeed the world, to receive the same blessed assurance he

---

[11]A key issue in King studies concerns the roots of King's thought. As noted by Clayborne Carson, "Martin Luther King, Jr., and the African-American Social Gospel," in *African-American Religion*, 349, recent studies have tended to emphasize the roots of King's thought, including his theology, in African American religious traditions—an emphasis intended to counter earlier King studies that focused almost exclusively on European American influences. William Watley's succinct statement captures the more recent trend well: "Although Dr. King was a leader of all people, he was uniquely and peculiarly the product of the black community—and, more specifically, the black church." See "A Black Hero for All People," *Christian Century* 2 (January 15, 1986): 39. Watley's statement followed two key articles by James H. Cone ("Martin Luther King, Jr.: Black Theology—Black Church," *Theology Today* 40 [January 1984]: 409–12; and "Black Theology in American Religion," *Journal of the American Academy of Religion* 53, no. 4 [December 1985]: 755–71) in which he argues that King derived his religious beliefs and practices from the black faith. Others have made similar arguments. See, for example, Lewis V. Baldwin, *There Is a Balm in Gilead: The Cultural Roots of Martin Luther King, Jr.* (Minneapolis: Fortress Press, 1991); Luther Ivory, *Toward a Theology of Radical Involvement*; Lischer, *The Preacher King*; Thomas Mikelson, "The Negro's God in the Theology of Martin Luther King, Jr.: Social Community and Theological Discourse" (Th.D. diss., Harvard University, 1988); and Miller, *Voice of Deliverance*. Miller's thesis, as stated in an earlier article ("Martin Luther King, Jr., and the Black Folk Pulpit," 120–23), is especially instructive here: "Biographers and academics have persistently claimed that King's reading of famous Euro-American philosophers (especially G. W. F. Hegel) and theologians (especially Walter Rauschenbusch, Reinhold Niebuhr, and Paul Tillich) inspired his thought and his language and thus the civil rights movement. This view is wrong...King's worldview and discourse sprang from two major sources: the sermons of Harry Emerson Fosdick and other liberal white preachers, and the African-American folk pulpit of King's father and grandfather, both of whom were folk preachers." In Michael G. Long, *Against Us, But for Us: Martin Luther King, Jr., and the State* (Macon, Ga.: Mercer University Press, 2002), I have argued that the question of whether King's roots are in either African American or European American traditions presents a false dilemma. The roots of King's thought are in both—in the Black Baptist church, for example, and in the theological liberalism he encountered through white preachers and theologians. Still, with indebtedness to Douglas Sturm, "Martin Luther King, Jr., as Democratic Socialist," *Journal of Religious Ethics* 18 (Fall 1990): 84, I have also argued that, though King's thought had many roots, it was *ultimately* rooted in his African American experiences, especially those with his family, friends, and Morehouse professors.

had felt deep in his heart during the kitchen epiphany—the assurance of the abiding, and empowering, presence of God in Jesus.

When we have this assurance, King preached, we can move through all of time without any lasting fear. Yes, of course, fear will come upon us in intense moments of redemptive suffering, but if we have faith in God-with-us, if we trust that God will never desert us, if we believe that we are never alone, no, never alone, we can plant our feet on the ground, hold our heads in the air, and ultimately fear no one who tries to come between us and God in our efforts to live creatively. "Because," as King put it, "you know that God is even in Crete. If you ascend to the heavens, God is there. If you descend to hell, God is even there. If you take the wings of the morning and fly out to the uttermost parts of the sea, even God is there. Everywhere we turn we find him. We can never escape him."[12]

These words, preached shortly before his 1968 death, reveal King's firm conviction that God is everywhere and with everyone— that God is, as King had put it five years earlier, "the ground and essence of all reality."[13] Even as a student, King had expressed frustration with European theologians, including Karl Barth, who seemed to depict God, at least on occasion, as wholly transcendent, wholly separate from temporal life, wholly divorced from everyday experience. Identifying himself as a liberal theologian, King had written that, unlike the theologians of transcendence, the liberal "sees the light of God shining through history as the blossom shines through the bud: God is working through history."[14]

It was not just theologians like Barth that incurred King's theological wrath, though; it was also materialist philosophies like communism. Deeply critical of the materialist dimension of

[12]King, "Unfulfilled Dreams," *Knock*, 200.

[13]Martin Luther King Jr., "How Should a Christian View Communism," in *Strength to Love* (Philadelphia: Fortress Press, 1981), 97. This phrase is indebted to the theology of Paul Tillich, one of the key subjects of King's dissertation at Boston University.

[14]Martin Luther King Jr., "The Sources of Fundamentalism and Liberalism Considered Historically and Psychologically," *Called to Serve: January 1929–June 1951*, vol. 1 of *The Papers of Martin Luther King, Jr.*, ed. Clayborne Carson et al. (Berkeley: University of California Press, 1992), 239. King's liberalism, which is distinctly different from the relatively conservative theology of Daddy King, has two primary branches: the social gospel tradition preached by Benjamin Mays, and the formal personalist tradition King embraced during his years in seminary and

communism, King argued in 1958 that history is guided not by matter but by the Spirit of God: History is pregnant with the divine, full of meaning, love, justice, order, and power. [15]

In King's view, then, we should not even begin to contemplate fleeing history and escaping to the heavens above in order to experience the empowering presence of God for creative living. All we need to do is stay right here, in this time and place, open ourselves in prayerful attitude, and receive the One from whom we cannot escape, especially when we feel we are on the brink of failure at a kitchen table in the middle of the loneliest night of our lives.

---

graduate school. In short, personalism is a school of thought that posits God as personal and the human personality as the starting point for understanding all reality. For more on the complicated relationship between King and personalism, see Rufus Burrow Jr., "Personalism, the Objective Moral Order, and Moral Law in the Work of Martin Luther King, Jr.," in *The Legacy of Martin Luther King, Jr.: The Boundaries of Law, Politics, and Religion* (Notre Dame, Ind.: University of Notre Dame Press, 2002), 213–51. Even though King identified himself as a liberal, however, Richard Lischer, *The Preacher King*, 53, questions the depth of King's commitment to liberalism. As Lischer puts it, "No matter how many times he repeated the liberal platitudes about the laws of human nature, morality, and history, King could not *be* a liberal because liberalism's Enlightenment vision of the harmony of humanity, nature, and God skips a step that is essential to the development of black identity. It has little experience of the evil and suffering borne by enslaved and segregated people in America." However, Lischer's definition of liberalism is a bit limited: after all, Mays's liberalism, born to rebel, accounted for the evil and suffering Lisher notes. Finally, with King's identification as a theological liberal in mind, I think John W. Rathbun overstated his point when he argued that "King does not particularly care which philosophical or theological terms are used to describe God," in "Martin Luther King: The Theology of Social Action," *American Quarterly* 20 (Spring 1968): 42. It was evident, even in 1968, that King took special care in avoiding terms such as "impersonal," "warrior," and "vengeful" when describing God. Rathbun nods at this point, but does not make enough of it when characterizing King's doctrine of God.

[15]Martin Luther King Jr., *Stride Toward Freedom: The Montgomery Story* (New York: Harper & Row, 1958), 92. King understood communism as a "protest against unfair treatment of the poor," but also as a system wrongly devoted to materialism, ethical relativism, and political totalitarianism. Miller, *Voice of Deliverance*, 101–4, notes that King borrowed his double attitude toward communism from Robert McCracken, *Questions People Ask* (New York: Harper & Brothers, 1951), 163–72. For more on King and communism, see Adam Fairclough, "Was Martin Luther King a Marxist?" *History Workshop* 15 (Spring 1983): 117–25. In a 1966 speech to his staff, King opposed both "the rugged individualism of capitalism and the impersonal collectivism of communism," embracing instead the earthly expression of the reign of God—democratic socialism. See Martin Luther King Jr., "Speech to Staff Retreat at Frogmore, South Carolina, 14 November 1966," King Center and Archives, Atlanta.

God Is Mother and Father

For King, God is immanent, always present, in the time of our life together, and God is present not just in any way, but in a deeply personal way. God is not a disinterested being who created the world and then left it to its own devices, or a supernatural power out of touch with the individual personalities of creation, or an impersonal ground of being we cannot talk with, hear from, and even love. "God," King wrote in graduate school, "is a conscious Person of eternal duration."[16] God hears, talks, feels, and thinks.

King sketched a rationale for this belief in his Boston University dissertation. "In the world of experiences," he wrote, "the basic source of personality production and sustenance has been personality. Now when we are confronted with the fact of personality production and sustenance on a cosmic scale, why not ascribe the source to cosmic personality?"[17] In addition, King suggested that, because goodness presupposes freedom and intelligence—characteristics of personality—and because real love can happen only between people, God must be a conscious person. Otherwise, we could not speak of either the goodness of God or the possibility of communion with God.[18]

For King, God has personality, and just because God is deeply personal, we can and should enter into a relationship with God and thereby experience the comfort and empowerment that only God can offer. In his own deeply personal relationship with God, King believed that he had discovered the intimacy one can feel within the bonds of a loving family. "He's my everything," King preached in 1963. "He's my mother and my father. He's my sister and my brother. He's a friend to the friendless."[19] Far from impersonal, God

---

[16]The words are actually King's description of Edgar Sheffield Brightman's understanding of God—an understanding with which King was, in his own words, "quite sympathetic." See King, "Final Examination Answers, Philosophy of Religion," *Rediscovering Precious Values, July 1951–November 1955*, vol. 2 of *The Papers of Martin Luther King, Jr.*, ed. Clayborne Carson et al. (Berkeley: University of California Press, 1994), 109.

[17]King, "A Comparison of the Conceptions of God in the Thinking of Paul Tillich and Henry Nelson Wieman," *Papers*, 2: 510. At this point King was critiquing Paul Tillich's "supra-personal" God, a God without consciousness and rationality.

[18]Ibid., 513–14.

[19]King, "The Three Dimensions of a Complete Life," *Knock*, 139.

is the father and mother who create, redeem, and sustain us; God is the brother and sister who hold our hands as we face the fears they have already overcome; and God is the friend who sits with us at the kitchen table as we drown our most intimate worries in yet another cup of coffee. King stated this same belief, but much more formally, in his 1963 book of sermons:

> To say that God is personal is not to make him a finite object beside other objects or attribute to him the limitations of human personality; it is to take what is finest and noblest in our consciousness and affirm its perfect existence in him. It is certainly true that human personality is limited, but personality as such involves no necessary limitations. It means simply self-consciousness and self-direction. So in the truest sense of the word, God is a living God. In him there is feeling and will, responsive to the deepest yearnings of the human heart: *this* God both evokes and answers prayer.[20]

It is thus quite clear that King's God was the God of traditional theism. Indeed, King confessed as much: "I feel," he wrote in his student years, "that the most valid conception of God is theism."[21] Although he did not define it when he wrote these words, by "theism" King meant his belief in a God who is personal, supernatural, and able to intervene in human history at will.[22] This belief in a theistic God formed as he first listened to the sermons of Daddy King, and then became even more compelling to King as he studied theism at seminary and graduate school and, most importantly, as he prayed at the kitchen table and felt assured that the living God directly intervened in the time of his life to offer him—Martin Luther King Jr.—the strength and courage he needed to move from a life of despair to a life of creativity. This personal God, he believed, can do the exact same thing for us.

[20]King, *Strength to Love*, 141–42.
[21]King, *Papers*, 1: 290.
[22]This tidy definition of traditional theism is found in John Shelby Spong, *Why Christianity Must Change or Die: A Bishop Speaks to Believers in Exile* (San Francisco: Harper SanFrancisco, 1998), 46.

The Highest Revelation of God

King hoped that no one would go through time without encountering and experiencing the God who has chosen to be in time so that *all* of humanity can have the strength and courage it needs for creative living. "Remember," he would often witness to his friends, "God lives!"[23] The living God whom King had in mind was the God he found to be present in Jesus of Nazareth. As he put it in reply to an *Ebony* reader who had asked about Jesus: "He, more than any other person that has ever lived in history, reveals the true nature of God. Through his life, death, and resurrection, the power of eternity broke forth into time." And because he reveals the true nature of God, and thereby allows eternal love to break forth into mundane time, Jesus is the Christ—not just any revelation of God, but "the highest revelation of God."[24]

King did not mean to suggest that God did not arrive in time until Jesus' life, death, and resurrection, but rather that through Jesus the power of the divine became more clearly revealed in time than ever before. King also believed that Jesus continues in this present

---

[23]King, "To Fred L. Shuttlesworth," *Birth of a New Age, December 1955–December 1956,* vol. 3 of *The Papers of Martin Luther King, Jr.,* ed. Clayborne Carson et al. (Berkeley: University of California Press, 1997), 496.

[24]King, "Advice for Living," *Symbol of the Movement, January 1957–December 1958,* vol. 4 of *The Papers of Martin Luther King, Jr.,* ed. Clayborne Carson et al. (Berkeley: University of California Press, 2000), 472. King believed that Jesus revealed the true nature of God by surrendering himself to God and developing a consciousness that was unique in its understanding of God. King expressed this belief most clearly in his reply, in "Advice for Living" (*Papers,* 4: 279–80), to someone who asked about the reason for God's decision to "make Jesus white." King replied: "The color of Jesus' skin is of little or no consequence…The significance of Jesus lay, not in His color, but in His unique God-consciousness and His willingness to surrender His will to God's will. He was the Son of God, not because of His external biological makeup, but because of His internal spiritual commitment. He would have been no more significant if His skin had been black. He is no less significant because His skin was white." For more on the christology of King, see Jon M. Temme, "Jesus as Trailblazer: The christology of Martin Luther King, Jr.," *Journal of Religious Thought* 42 (Spring-Summer 1985): 75–80; and L. Harold DeWolf, "Martin Luther King, Jr., as Theologian," *Journal of the Interdenominational Theological Center* 4 (Spring 1977): 1–11. DeWolf rightly notes that King's reference to the unique God-consciousness of Jesus has a direct connection to the christology of Schleiermacher (3).

moment to reveal and make real the presence of God in time. Remembering the kitchen epiphany, King held that Jesus is not just a historical figure lurking in the past; the Spirit of Jesus lives today, assuring us that we will never be alone, no, never alone in our struggles for love and justice, and empowering us to stand up for what is right. Just so, in King's thought, it is not God in general who makes creative living possible; it is the God in Jesus who can empower us for creative living by giving us the wisdom and strength we so desperately need.

As Jesus is not a figure stuck in the past, neither is he a quiet man who is now adorned in flowing white robes, sitting next to the throne of God the Creator in heaven. King never understood Jesus to be a lily-white angelic figure holding a golden staff while overlooking the vast creation beneath him, waiting, just waiting for the judgment day. Rather, King found Jesus to be present right here, right now, in the messiness of earthly time.

King's own experience suggested that we can most clearly encounter the Spirit of Jesus in "the least of these," the downtrodden of society. In Matthew 25, one of King's favorite biblical passages, the Son of Man carries out the Great Judgment by rewarding those who cared for "the least"—the hungry, the thirsty, the stranger, the naked, the sick, and the imprisoned—and cursing those who ignored them. Matthew even reports the Son of Man as saying, "'Truly I tell you, just as you did it to one of the least of these who are members of my family, you did it to me'" (Mt. 25:40).

King took this text to heart, perhaps more than any other, and closely followed Matthew in identifying the Spirit of Jesus to be among the marginalized, those far removed from earthly comfort. Further, King used this text to give substance to his understanding of the practices of creative living. Inspired by Matthew 25, King understood creative living to mean nothing less than actively reflecting the will of Jesus—feeding the hungry, giving drink to the thirsty, and comforting the afflicted.

With the Matthean Jesus in mind, King held a special place in his heart for people who cared for those on the underside of history, and he wanted the caretakers to trust that their creative work placed them directly in the presence of the God revealed in Jesus. Consider the end of a sermon he delivered to his beloved Ebenezer congregation in 1966:

It seems that I can hear the God of the universe smiling and speaking to his church, saying, "You are a great church because I was hungry and ye fed me. You are a great church (*Glory to God*) because I was naked and ye clothed me. You are a great church because I was sick and ye visited me. You are a great church because I was in prison and ye gave me consolation by visiting me." (*Yes, sir*) And this is the church that's going to save this world.[25]

Interestingly, King used this same text as an indictment against the United States, preaching that because America does not feed the hungry and clothe the naked, it "cannot enter the kingdom of greatness."[26] Clearly, though, both of his uses of this text—affirmative and condemnatory—point to King's strong sense that we can find the Spirit of Jesus, in this time, by being with "the least of these." King would say that there is no need for us to leave earthly time in our spiritual quest to tap into the source of creative living: All we need to do is find the poor, the destitute, the lepers, and the imprisoned and help create better conditions for them so that they might flourish, for where "the least of these" are is exactly where we can find the creative Spirit of God as revealed in Jesus.

Cosmic Companionship

Because he was jailed so many times, King was especially comforted by Jesus' identification with the imprisoned, and he firmly believed that the God revealed in Jesus continues to be present with the righteous saints who find themselves behind bars because of their witness to the love of God. About his own jail experience in Birmingham in 1963, King wrote, "I had never truly been in solitary confinement. God's companionship does not stop at the door of a jail cell. God had been my cellmate."[27]

To be sure, King believed that God, as the ground and essence of all reality, is with everyone and everything, but he also stressed that the presence of the personal God revealed in Jesus is especially assured to those who struggle for love, justice, and peace, and against

---

[25]King, "Guidelines for a Constructive Church," *Knock*, 114–15.
[26]King, *Autobiography*, 354.
[27]Ibid., 186.

all forms of evil. God, King wrote in 1963, "is not outside the world looking on with a sort of cold indifference. Here on all the roads of life, he is striving in our striving...the God of the universe struggles with us."[28] By "us," King clearly meant those who struggle to make the will of God come alive in history, particularly those active in the civil rights movement. "God walks with us," he proclaimed to his followers.[29] Yes, the struggle will sometimes overwhelm us, but nothing can overwhelm the presence of God in the time of our righteous struggles. Whenever we struggle for right and good, whenever we push the reign of God farther along, whenever we stand against the forces of evil, we can be assured of "cosmic companionship"—the one and only companionship that empowers us to live creatively.[30]

King did not believe that his sense of "cosmic companionship" in the struggle for human freedom was anything new: "This is the long faith of the Hebraic-Christian tradition: that God is not some Aristotelian 'unmoved mover' who merely contemplates upon Himself. He is not merely a self-knowing God, but an other-loving God forever working through history for the establishment of His kingdom."[31]

King's unwavering sense of "cosmic companionship" was perhaps most visible when he spoke of little boys and girls who struggled for freedom even though they had never studied all the philosophical debates about procedural and substantive freedom. When he preached his brief, yet deeply moving, sermon upon the death of four little girls in a Montgomery church bombing in 1963, it was impossible not to sense his unwavering belief that God was with the girls in their final moments of life here on earth. And when he stood among the children of Birmingham who withstood the violence of local police thugs, with their vicious dogs and fire hoses, he led the crowds to feel that no one other than God was holding the hands of the little children as they walked directly into harm's way—and jail.

---

[28]King, "The Death of Evil Upon the Seashore," *Strength*, 83.

[29]King, "Our God Is Able," *Strength*, 110.

[30]Martin Luther King Jr., "Nonviolence and Racial Justice," in *A Testament of Hope: The Essential Writings and Speeches of Martin Luther King, Jr.*, ed. James M. Washington (San Francisco: Harper SanFrancisco, 1986), 9.

[31]Martin Luther King Jr., "Give Us the Ballot," in *A Call to Conscience: The Landmark Speeches of Dr. Martin Luther King, Jr.*, ed. Clayborne Carson and Kris Shepard (New York: Warner Books, 2001), 54.

God Saves the Murderer

King's God, then, is not encapsulated in the eternal heaven, but is walking, right now, with little boys and girls, and adult women and men, who sacrifice their own lives in creative living. Still, though he emphasized God's presence with the civil rights activists, King never sought to restrict the presence of God, and he certainly never wanted us to believe that the God of history is present merely with those who struggle for good. God may favor the work of those who struggle, but God is never found merely on one side of the struggle. God never divides and destroys the creation, but God creates and builds up all of creation.

Rather than claiming that God is with "us" but not "them," King hoped that we could sense the presence of God even with our enemies. Our enemies, as he saw them, are never wholly depraved, or wholly outside the love of God. Just like us, even our worst enemies, no matter who they are and what they have done, have the image of God within them and so are able to see and do the good before them.[32]

And because the image of God is within them, we should never write them off as if they are merely children of evil: God loves even the most evil enemies and intends for their conversion and reconciliation. King expressed this belief, among other places, in reply to an *Ebony* reader who asked if he believed that God approves the death penalty for crimes like rape and murder:

> I do not think that God approves the death penalty for any crime—rape and murder included. God's concern is to improve individuals and bring them to the point of conversion…Shall a good God harbor resentment? Since the purpose of jailing a criminal is that of reformation rather than retribution…it is highly inconsistent to take the life of a criminal…Capital punishment is against the best judgment of modern criminology and, above all, against the highest expression of love in the nature of God.[33]

---

[32]The third chapter will devote more attention to the practice of loving your enemies.

[33]King, "Advice for Living," *Papers,* 4: 305.

If we are to discover the God of history, then, we would do well to be not only with those we know and love as family and friends, but also with those who hate and despise us. Because the love of God, the source of creative living, is with our enemies, we can grow significantly by being present to and with them, seeking not to kill them, even for crimes like rape and murder, but to reform them in light of the image of God within them. More pointedly, we can grow significantly by struggling against the work of our enemies, and the systems that support such work, in our pursuit of divine justice. This last point, as the following chapters will highlight, is especially critical: For King, creative growth comes not through a life free of conflict but especially through a life of struggle against evil and for the good.

God Is Love

In King's view, the God of history has left a divine mark not only within people, including "the least of these," as well as our enemies, but also on the world, especially by creating it with distinct moral laws. Influenced by the social gospel movement, King believed that as the physical world is governed by God-given laws (for example, the law of gravity), so too is the moral world governed by divine principles. Christianity, he stated, "sets forth a system of absolute moral values and affirms that God has placed within the structure of this universe certain moral principles that are fixed and immutable."[34] An example of a moral absolute in King's thought is the principle that the end does not justify the means; the end and the means must always cohere in creative living.

Whatever the principle may be, though, it is certain to reflect the law of love, the primary imperative of the moral order of the universe. As King put it in 1956, love is "the heartbeat of the moral cosmos."[35] As the center of morality, love is also the center of creative

---

[34]King, "How Should a Christian View Communism?" *Strength*, 98. King was long familiar with the concept of moral laws. He studied the concept in seminary and graduate school, but he most likely first heard about them from Benjamin Mays, who spoke of the "ethical laws" of the universe. See Benjamin E. Mays, *Born to Rebel* (New York: Charles Scribner's Sons, 1971), 196.

[35]King, "Paul's Letter to American Christians," *Papers*, 3: 420.

living: Creativity flows from the presence of love, makes love real in the here and now, and returns to love for more power.

When explaining what he meant by love, King turned primarily to the cross of Jesus, the place where he believed he discovered the highest form of love—the love of God breaking forth into time. In King's view, Jesus suffered unflinchingly on the cross, sacrificing his own life and forgiving his accusers along the way, so that humanity might forever be drawn closer to one another and to the God of love. And doing so, Jesus revealed the essence of divine love (*agape*) to be nonviolent, sacrificial in its unselfishness, forgiving, reconciling, and so powerful that it endures beyond death.[36] Embodying this type of love, the most durable power in the world, Jesus revealed the very heart of creative living—to love as he loved.

For King, whenever we practice this cruciform love, the agapeic love of Jesus, a love that seeks nothing in return, we encounter God: "As John says, 'God is love.' He who loves is a participant in the being of God."[37] Thus, to experience God is to love as Jesus loved—always sacrificing ourselves for others, forgiving others seventy times seven, seeking reconciliation with any and all we are estranged from, and being ever nonviolent in our efforts to mold our personal character and create social justice.[38] In King's thought, enacting cruciform love relentlessly is creative living at its best, and just so, it is also deeply sacramental in character: God is here, right now, in the giving and receiving of cruciform love.

God Is Justice

But King did not hold that God is merely love—he was convinced that God is also justice, and that justice is a key part of the moral order that God has created. By positing both love and justice within both the character of God and the moral order of the universe, King suggested that love and justice are deeply connected and that each supplements the other. Creative living is thus embracing,

---

[36]For more on King's notion of cruciform love, see Long, *Against Us, But for Us*, 100–106.

[37]King, "The Most Durable Power in the World," *Testament*, 11.

[38]The following chapters will explain in greater detail the significance of love and justice for the practices of creative living.

embodying, and enacting both love and justice, not just one or the other.[39]

King gave different content to his understanding of the substance of justice throughout his life, but there are a few constants worth noting for our practice of creative living. As a student at Boston University, he had clearly stated his agreement with the prophet Amos' belief that God despises those who trample on the poor in an effort to acquire personal wealth. The justice of God, in this view, requires that the poor receive the basic goods they need to survive. King preached this material sense of divine justice throughout his life, and it came to expression especially when he addressed Matthew 25, as noted above.

But King's notion of justice also had another constant dimension—punishment. King's just God is no soft sentimentalist but a firm judge who hones in on sin and sinners, demands repentance, and punishes those who show no repentance for having broken the laws of the moral universe. Consider the words King spoke at the first meeting of the Montgomery Improvement Association, called together to protest the arrest of Rosa Parks:

> The Almighty God himself is not…only…the God just standing up saying through Hosea, "I love you, Israel." He's also the God that stands up before nations and said [*sic*]: "Be still and know that I am God, that if you don't obey me I

---

[39]For more on the relationship between love and justice in King's thought, see Greg Moses, *Revolution of Conscience: Martin Luther King, Jr., and the Philosophy of Nonviolence* (New York: The Guilford Press, 1997), 185–226; and Preston Williams, "An Analysis of the Conception of Love and Justice in the Thought of Martin Luther King, Jr.," *The Journal of Religious Ethics* 18 (Fall 1990): 15–31. An excellent article on King's thought on justice in light of the work of John Rawls is Robert Michael Franklin, "In Pursuit of a Just Society: Martin Luther King, Jr., and John Rawls," *Journal of Religious Ethics* 18 (Fall 1990): 57–77. See also Franklin's book, *Liberating Visions: Human Fulfillment and Social Justice in African-American Thought* (Minneapolis: Fortress Press, 1990). Finally, an interesting early article is James E. Sellers, "Love, Justice, and the Nonviolent Method," *Theology Today* 18 (January 1962): 422–34.

will break the backbone of your power and slap you out of the orbits of your international and national relationships."[40]

The just God, in this view, is judge and executioner. These two dimensions of justice are also related in King's thought—the just God judges and punishes those who fail to care for the poor and downtrodden.[41] Further, God does not reserve concern for the poor, or judgment and punishment, merely for the life hereafter. God, in other words, does not offer a pie in the sky without any slices here; nor does God refuse pie to evildoers only after they die. God demands and commands justice *now*.

And so should we. For King, creative living is a life that demands justice in the here and now. If we are to live creatively, we must never forget the poor, as most people do, but actively serve them not only by seeking economic justice, but also by seeking to restrain those who would break laws on the backs of the poor.

Wherever we do this, wherever we find or establish justice, we encounter God, because God *is* justice. So King would counsel against setting our eyes solely on the prize, a reward in the by-and-by. Participate in justice now, he would say, and we will discover the God of history in the time of our life.

God Is One

Because King believed that God has created the world with physical laws, such as the law of gravity, and moral laws, which include the principles of love and justice, he also held that the time of our life has an underlying order. Indeed, King saw our entire life as divinely ordered.

Yes, our life may seem terribly chaotic at times, but it never really is. As King put it in 1963: "Beneath and above the shifting sands of time, the uncertainties that darken our days, and the

---

[40]King, "MIA Mass Meeting at Holt Street Baptist Church," *Papers*, 3: 73–74. Note the prophetic rage in King's words. With these words in mind, I oppose King scholars who have suggested that King did not rely on prophetic rage until after the Selma movement. (See, for example, Lischer, *The Preacher King*, 11, 180–81.) King assumed the role of prophet—even the angry prophet—long before the last three years of his life.
[41]For more on King's notion of divine justice, see Long, *Against Us, But for Us*, 107–12.

vicissitudes that cloud our nights is a wise and loving God." Of course, this wise and loving God is the One who provides our life with order: "The universe is not a tragic expression of meaningless chaos but a marvelous display of orderly cosmos...Above the manyness of time stands the one eternal God, with wisdom to guide us, strength to protect us, and love to keep us."[42]

For King, then, our responsibility as believers is not to let the craziness of life wear us down and destroy us as we seek love and justice. Instead, our vocation is to believe what we cannot see, and to trust that, in spite of the apparent chaos, our life is in good order—an order established by the God of stability. With the kitchen experience ever in his heart and mind, King maintained that creative living depends on our willingness to trust that God is in control even in those moments when evil seems to overwhelm and undermine our quest for love and justice.

God Is Able

Further, King believed that the eternal God of love, justice, and order also has power, "boundless power," as he put it, to guide, protect, and keep us.[43] God is able "to sustain the vast scope of the physical universe";[44] God is able "to subdue all the powers of evil";[45] God is able "to give us interior resources to confront the trials and difficulties of life";[46] and God is able "to make a way out of no way, and transform dark yesterdays into bright tomorrows."[47]

God, King preached in 1963, is not an "omnipotent czar," an "absolute sovereign," a "despot," or an "almighty dictator" who controls every dimension of our life with "Gestapo-like methods."[48] Though King suggested in his dissertation that he affirmed the omnipotence of God, he was clear to specify what he meant by divine omnipotence: "It does not mean that God can do the non-doable...It means, rather, that God has the power to actualize the

[42]King, "Antidotes for Fear," *Strength*, 124.
[43]King, "How Should a Christian View Communism," *Strength*, 97.
[44]King, "Our God Is Able," *Strength*, 108.
[45]Ibid., 109.
[46]Ibid., 111.
[47]Ibid., 114.
[48]King, "The Answer to a Perplexing Question," *Strength*, 132–33.

good and realize his purpose."[49] And God does this by joining us in the struggle for good and empowering us to find a way out of no way: God is able to help us do what is right, especially when we cannot find the right thing to do, and with the power of God to guide us, we can indeed move on to a brighter tomorrow.

This is exactly what creative living is all about—accepting power from God in the midnight of life to move into and create the positive future that God intends for us. We can do this best, according to King, by mirroring God's own practice of creating power—joining hands with the people of God so that together we can overcome the evil that seeks to separate us from ourselves, others, and God. In this sense, creative living finds power in *community*—the people of God who engage in the struggle against evil and for good.

The Beloved Community

King also believed that the God of love, justice, and order empowers us for a purpose—to lead us to freedom. Reflecting the black church's emphasis on the Exodus story, King claimed that freedom is the essence, the distinguishing mark, the inner core, of all humanity.[50] For King, freedom means "one's capacity to deliberate, decide and respond" for oneself, and its absence "is the imposition of restraint on my deliberation as to what I shall do, where I shall

[49]King, "A Comparison of the Conceptions of God in the Thinking of Paul Tillich and Henry Nelson Wieman," *Papers,* 2:525–26.

[50]For more on King and the exodus story, see James H. Smylie, "On Jesus, Pharaohs, and the Chosen People: Martin Luther King as Biblical Interpreter and Humanist," *Interpretation* 24 (January 1970): 74–91. See also Miller, *Voice of Deliverance,* 169–85. Both of these pieces also deal with King's understanding of himself in light of Moses. "King," Smylie writes, "did not want to be like Moses...King wanted to be more and more like Jesus" (76). Writing about King's last speech, however, Miller observes that King went beyond comparing himself to Moses: "[King] boldly equates himself with Moses at the end of the Hebrews' forty-year trek through the wilderness" (181–82). With the strength of Miller's argument in mind, I would simply contend that Smylie understates his point: King wanted to be like Moses *and* Jesus.

live, how much I shall earn, the kind of tasks I shall pursue."[51] King
did not believe that God wants us to be free from others; true freedom
is not freedom to be left alone. Rather, it is the opportunity for us to
achieve and enjoy a solid education, a well-paying job, decent health
care, and adequate housing—all the basic goods required for living
in an integrated and peaceful community where each individual is
affirmed as an equal member of the one family of God.[52]

Indeed, true freedom is the opportunity for us to live in "the
beloved community" that God in Jesus intends for all humanity.[53]
As King put it in 1956, the beloved community is a world in which
"men will live together as brothers; a world in which men will no
longer take from the masses to give luxuries to the classes. A world
in which men will throw down the sword and live by the higher
principle of love."[54] This brief statement, though made early in his
career, reveals the three constant dimensions of King's vision of the
beloved community that God desires: reconciliation, economic justice,
and nonviolent love.

---

[51]King, "The Ethical Demands for Integration," *Testament*, 92. Given King's
emphasis on love, especially in statements about the beloved community, it is clear
why Walter Earl Fluker has argued the following: "Although King's conception of
the 'beloved community' represents a synthesis from a wide range of thinkers, a
simple working definition is 'a community ordered by love.' Simply stated,
'community' refers to integration, mutuality, and harmony. 'Love' refers to the
Christian conception of *agape,*" in "They Looked for a City: A Comparison of the
Idea of Community in Howard Thurman and Martin Luther King, Jr.," *Journal of
Religious Ethics* 18(Fall 1990): 39. Still, given the deliberate emphasis on economic
justice, I believe that a better short working definition is "a community ordered by
love and justice."

[52]Martin Luther King Jr., "The Birth of a New Age," *Papers*, 3: 344.

[53]I write "God in Jesus" to emphasize the Jesus-centric dimension to the beloved
community, and I intend for this emphasis to supplement Frederick L. Downing's
description of the beloved community as "theocentric" in "Martin Luther King, Jr.,
as Public Theologian," *Theology Today* 44 (April 1987): 180. King's vision of the
beloved community—with its integration, economic justice, and peace—is grounded
in his understanding of Jesus as one who loved without borders, ministered with
"the least of these," and embraced nonviolence. For a helpful article on the beloved
community, especially on its relationship to imagery of the reign of God, see John
H. Cartwright, "The Social Eschatology of Martin Luther King, Jr.," in *Essays in
Honor of Martin Luther King, Jr.*, ed. John H. Cartwright (Evanston, Ill.: Garrett
Theological Seminary, 1977), 1–13; see also Kenneth L. Smith and Ira G. Zepp Jr.,
Search for the Beloved Community: The Thinking of Martin Luther King, Jr. (Valley Forge,
Pa.: Judson Press, 1974).

[54]King, "The Birth of a New Age," *Papers*, 3: 344.

King knew that there are serious obstructions to the beloved community, and he clearly identified them as the three interrelated evils of racism, economic injustice, and militarism, all of which degrade the human personality and create artificial barriers between equal members of the human family. Given the presence of these obstructions, he conceded that we will not enjoy full freedom—a time of reconciliation—until the world experiences "a revolution of values"—the day when integration, economic justice, and peace emerge within the world.[55] In other words, we will not enjoy full freedom until humanity experiences the reconciliation that God in Jesus intends for all humanity.

Until the beloved community arrives, we will continue to reside in broken communities, with just glimpses of the daybreak of freedom. But the God who enters time is with us even, and perhaps especially, in our broken communities: Wherever and whenever freedom breaks through broken lives, there is God. Pushing broken lives toward the wholeness of freedom is exactly what God does, and there is no time in the experience of our life when God is not fighting for our freedom within the beloved community. As King put it in 1957, "…God is working in this world, and at this hour, and at this moment."[56] Every moment of our lives God is working to clear the way to the promised land.

[55]For more on the revolution of values, see Martin Luther King Jr., *Where Do We Go from Here: Chaos or Community?* (Boston: Beacon Press, 1968). In response to this book, as well as others, John Rathbun argued that "King is not entirely clear as to what his 'revolution' entails," in "Martin Luther King: The Theology of Social Action," 51. Many others have joined Rathbun through the years in criticizing King for a lack of policy specifics, but I believe they're wrong. Regarding integration, King recommended specific policies on such issues as transportation, education, housing, even the awarding of federal housing contracts. Indeed, King offered JFK specific policy recommendations in a document titled "An Appeal to the Honorable John F. Kennedy, President of the United States, for National Rededication to the Principles of Emancipation Proclamation and for an Executive Order Prohibiting Segregation in the United States" (17 May 1962, King Archives). Regarding economic justice, I argued in my first King book that he clearly favored a welfare state like Sweden's—a democratic socialist state that would redistribute the wealth and ensure decent education, employment, health care, and pension security, among other things, for all citizens. And regarding peace, King was clear in his policy proposals for ending the Vietnam War, for nuclear disarmament, and for the integration of foreign policy teams. Thus, I suggest that, in comparison to other social activists who are not politicians, King was exceptionally specific in offering policy proposals and so exceptionally clear as to what his revolution entailed.

[56]King, "The Birth of a New Nation," *Call*, 40.

And our mission in life is to join God in creating the beloved community. For King, as the following chapters will highlight, the characteristics of the beloved community—integration, economic justice, and peace—provide us with *the* substance of creative living: Living creatively means creating the beloved community. No, we need not run away from our broken lives in order to encounter God, but what we must do is to fight for freedom now: fight for integration now, fight for economic justice now, and fight for peace now.[57] When we seek to create the beloved community, when we take steps toward the promised land, we join hearts and hands with the God who has entered the time of our life so that we can be empowered with wisdom and strength on our journey toward true freedom. Creating the beloved community, we meet the One who creates.

God Is in Nature

For King, then, God is *in* history—where there is love, justice, order, power, and freedom, there is God. The source of creative living is not in the heavens, inaccessible to us in our struggle to live creatively—God is here. But King would not stop with human history when pointing to signs of the creative presence of God in our lives; nor would he speak merely of God in Jesus when pointing to evidence of God. As a student, King had boldly suggested that, if we want evidence of God in our lives, we should look not only to humanity in general and to the Spirit of Jesus in particular, but also to the beauty of the natural world.

One of the little known facts about King is his deep appreciation for the natural world.[58] It was an appreciation that stemmed from far back in his life and came to regular expression during his seminary education, when he would make a daily trip "to commune with nature." "Every day," King wrote, "I would sit on the edge of the campus by the side of the river and watch the beauties of nature. My

---

[57]The third chapter will describe this practice in greater detail.

[58]This point is so little known because King did not emphasize it in later years. Indeed, during the civil rights movement, King focused on the God of history so much that he seemed to leave the God of nature totally behind. Nevertheless, the theme of God and nature appears in King's thought, and it would be negligent not to include the theme here.

friend, in this experience, I saw God. I saw him in birds of the air, the leaves of the tree, the movement of the rippling waves."[59]

This witness is considerably different from the one in which King spoke of the voice of Jesus, but his witness is no less clear. When he looked up at the stars, or watched the sunrise, or experienced the night moon, King always felt, in the deep recesses of his heart, that he saw not just nature but the God of nature. "There is God," he professed. God is in the stars, the sun, the moon. "Henry Ward Beecher was right: 'Nature is God's tongue.'"[60]

So, yet again, there is no need for us to run from the world in our spiritual quest to encounter the creativity of God. Instead, our calling is just to go for a walk, right here and right now, opening all of our senses to the beauty of the natural world around us. In this sense, creative living includes paying deep attention to the world of both history *and* nature. More exactly, though, it means paying attention to the *new* creations of God. King did not believe that God created the world a long time ago and then just stopped creating altogether. Rather, he believed in "creative evolution" and "emergent evolution." The God who created millions of years ago continues to create today and will continue to create tomorrow. "May it not be," King asked, "that God is creating from eternity?"[61] The question was rhetorical, because King held that "God is continually doing new and unpredictable things in the sequence of natural law. God is not a static dead God. He is a God who is alive today and will be forever more."[62] Just so, creative living is attentive, and responsive, to God's creation of "a new thing." Like the created world, then, creative living evolves: it changes in response to the changing dynamics of the world.

God Transcends

King recognized that there is potential danger in preaching just the radical immanence of God in history and nature—namely, the destructive possibility that his followers would equate present conditions with the will of God. Thus, though he argued that God

---

[59]King, *Autobiography*, 29.
[60]Ibid.
[61]King, "Examination Answers, Christian Theology for Today," *Papers*, 1: 291.
[62]Ibid., 294.

is "tender enough" to live in our lives, he also stressed that God is "tough-minded enough to transcend the world."[63] By embracing the doctrine of divine transcendence, King could thus refuse anyone who would dare to equate earthly conditions, especially segregation, poverty, and war, with the perfect will of God. Although God is in history, he could argue, history is not God—God is within and yet above history. On a related note, King also stressed that history holds humanity, and that because each person has potentialities for good and evil, history has always been "a struggle between good and evil."[64]

Thus, a key step in creative living is to point to the God above time in order to critique present times in our struggle to create the beloved community. The practical effect of divine transcendence, in other words, is that we can draw from the God above time in order to create a better world, and this, according to King, is exactly what we should do in our efforts to live creatively. In King's view, the world can always be a better place, and it is our responsibility to create this better world in accord with the transcendent will of God. But we should beware: Given the recalcitrance of human sin, which deepens within group life, evil never dies off willingly but only through a great struggle, especially with privileged groups.

God Is Eternal

Still, we should never lose heart. For King, the God of history will always prevail. Ultimately, history is the story of evil that advances only to be crushed by the God of justice.[65] Just because God is within the time of our life, working with us at every moment to establish the beloved community, we and others might fall pretty far back into animalistic ways at times, but "God controls the destiny of the universe, and Evil can't triumph in this universe."[66]

In King's view, evil was not at the beginning of the world; nor will it be at the end of time. In fact, neither evil nor anything else in all of creation can claim to be eternal. Interestingly, not even time,

---

[63]King, "A Tough Mind and a Tender Heart," *Strength*, 16.

[64]King, "Death of Evil," *Papers*, 3: 259.

[65]King's God is not magical, though. As the following chapter will note, King's God acts in history to triumph over evil, but this will take place only as people live out their allegiance to God rather than to human institutions.

[66]King, "Address to MIA Mass Meeting at Holt Street Baptist Church," *Papers*, 3: 200.

which is morally neutral, can claim to be eternal or endless, exactly because only God is eternal. To be sure, God enters the time of our life and includes all dimensions of time within the divine being, but God is in no way subject to the limitations of time—God is eternal. Given the eternity of God alone, King's advice is simple: We should give our allegiance not to the ravages of time but to the eternal God. As he put it in one of his earliest sermons:

> As a young man with most of my life ahead of me, I decided early (*Oh yeah*) on to give my life to something eternal and absolute. (*All right*) Not to these little gods that are here today and gone tomorrow. (*Come on*) But to God who is the same yesterday, today, and forever. *(Amen, Amen)*…That's the God that I call upon you to worship this morning. (*Yes*) Go out and be assured that that God is going to last forever. (*Yes*)…Plants may wither, the flowers may fade away, but the Word of our God shall stand forever, and nothing can ever stop Him. (*Bring it down*)[67]

Creative living, in King's thought, thus entails giving our allegiance to the one and eternal God—the God who is present to us not only in nature, but especially through history. The eternal God of love, justice, order, and power has chosen to enter the history of our life, right here and right now, to give us the strength and direction we need for traveling on the road to the promised land— a beloved community that reflects the love and justice found within the character of God. God's plan is to help us reach that beloved community, and, if we devote ourselves to creative living, God will not disappoint us—we will reach the promised land. In light of God's enduring presence, then, the best foundational work we can do, as we seek to live creatively, is to believe in and worship God, and to mirror the moral character of God in our own lives, trusting all the while that, as life dies around us, the source of creative power will never leave us alone, no, never alone, but will rise with us and lead us to a brighter tomorrow.

---

[67]King, "Rediscovering Lost Values," *Papers*, 2: 254–55.

CHAPTER TWO

Keep On Keeping On

Creative Living in the Past, Present, and Future

Because we have so often heard him recounting his dream of a brighter tomorrow—*I have a dream*—we most likely sense that King was a man focused on the future, when God would prevail by assuring the appearance of the beloved community in history. That sense is partly right, but it is also important for us to remember that King never lost sight of the past, nor did he seek to disengage himself from it, even as he dreamed of the beloved community of tomorrow.

Rather than focusing merely on the future, King sought to hold together the past, present, and future. On the one hand, he embraced all three as times of divine presence and as key parts of the beloved community. Because God is a God of history, God was in the past, God is in the present, and God will be in the future, and, just so, each temporal dimension is precious in its own right. On the other hand, King understood each as times of human sin and limitation, and as dangerous to the beloved community. King thus understood creative living as living in dialectical relationship to the time of our life. When we live creatively, in his view, we say both yes and no to the past, present, and future: We affirm part of each, but we also reject part of each.[1]

More Than a Dreamer

At the tender age of fourteen, King won an oratorical contest in Dublin, Georgia, with a speech that posed a direct challenge to the anemic democracy of the United States. The words of this speech, "The Negro and the Constitution," are stirring even today, sixty years after he first delivered them:

> We cannot have an enlightened democracy with one great group living in ignorance. We cannot have a healthy nation with one-tenth of the people ill-nourished…We cannot have a nation orderly and sound with one group so ground down and thwarted that it is almost forced into unsocial attitudes and crime…So as we gird ourselves to defend democracy from foreign attack, let us see to it that increasingly at home we give fair play and free opportunity for all people.[2]

On the bus trip home, the young King must have been dizzy from the heights of the day—a day when others had rightly recognized that this young man possessed skills rare among his peers. But the dizziness surely began to subside when the white bus driver ordered King and Sarah Grace Bradley, one of his favorite teachers, to give their seats to whites who had boarded the bus after they had. And the excitement certainly disappeared when the driver cursed King and his teacher for not surrendering their seats fast enough. "I intended to stay right in that seat," King recounted years later, "but Mrs. Bradley urged me up, saying we had to respect the law. We

---

[1]Because King studies have already given so much attention to the future that King dreamed of, I will devote the bulk of this chapter to his critical use of the past. The following chapters will then unpack King's plan for creative living in the present.

[2]Martin Luther King Jr., "The Negro and the Constitution," *Called to Serve: January 1929–June 1951,* vol. 1 of *The Papers of Martin Luther King, Jr.,* ed. Clayborne Carson et al. (Berkeley: University of California Press, 1992), 110. Note that even at this early age, King recognized a link between moral character and social systems—a link I will return to in the third chapter.

stood up in the aisle for ninety miles to Atlanta. *That night will never leave my memory.* It was the angriest I have ever been in my life."[3]

King remembered. His memory of the bus ride alone—*That night will never leave my memory*—suggests that it is wholly insufficient to characterize King as merely a man who dreamed of the future. More than a dreamer, King intentionally devoted a significant part of his life to the practice of remembering. Like the prophets of the Hebrew Scripture, who implored the Israelites to remember the Lord their God, King remembered because he believed that the past is an indispensable resource for creative living in the present and future.

No Past, No Future

"I find so many Negroes trying to be everything but a Negro," wrote a reader of King's advice column in 1958. "Why is the Negro so ashamed of his race? Why can't you find books about Negroes in the homes of Negroes?"[4] King was troubled by these questions enough to include them in his column, and his answer left no doubt as to his view on the fundamental significance of the past:

> The Negro must always guard against the danger of becoming ashamed of himself and his past. There is much in the heritage of the Negro that each of us can be proud of. The oppression that we have faced, partly because of the color of our skin, must not cause us to feel that everything nonwhite is objectionable. The content of one's character is the important thing, not the color of his skin. We must teach every Negro child that rejection of heritage means loss of cultural roots, *and people who have no past have no future.*[5]

---

[3] *The Autobiography of Martin Luther King, Jr.,* ed. Clayborne Carson (New York: Warner Books, 1998), 10 (emphasis mine).

[4] Martin Luther King Jr., "Advice for Living," *Symbol of the Movement, January 1957-December 1958,* vol. 4 of *The Papers of Martin Luther King, Jr.,* ed. Clayborne Carson et al. (Berkeley: University of California Press, 2000), 349.

[5] Ibid., 349–50 (emphasis mine). King was especially interested in helping African Americans remember their history of slavery, partly because he believed that the memory of emerging from slavery would give them inspiration to continue to struggle for civil rights. King often recounted the history of slavery in his sermons, noting, with more than a hint of gratitude to the slaves, that African Americans had come a long way since the endless years before the Civil War.

King understood the past to be a key part of one's personal and social identity. Our past is who we are—it is the very source of the people we have become and of the community that has given shape to our personalities. This means that to forget our past is to leave behind the resource we need for being ourselves today and becoming all we can be tomorrow. By ignoring our past, in King's view, we shut ourselves off from the creative source that gave us life, and thereby we undermine the creative potential of our present and future.

Going Backward to Go Forward

King embraced the past not only because of the experiential point that the past is the source of our present and future, but also because he believed that God was in the past, working graciously through people, nature, and events to bring about a brighter tomorrow. In one of his early sermons, "Rediscovering Lost Values," King reminded his listeners that God was "our help in ages past," a phrase drawn from the title of a popular Christian hymn.[6] And because God was in the past, King preached, "Sometimes, you know, it's necessary to go backward in order to go forward."[7]

King's homiletic point, taken from the story of Jesus left in the temple by his forgetful parents, was simple: We should not try to live in the present, or move boldly into the future, until we have gone back to the past and rediscovered the "mighty precious values" we have left behind—the God-given values that give meaning and purpose to our lives.[8]

As the first chapter noted, King envisioned the past as the time when God had created a universe with moral and spiritual laws that are relevant even in the present—for example, the moral law that

---

[6]King, "Rediscovering Lost Values," *Rediscovering Precious Values, July 1951–November 1955,* vol.2 of *The Papers of Martin Luther King, Jr.,* ed. Clayborne Carson et al. (Berkeley: University of California Press, 1994), 255. The title of the hymn is "O God, Our Help in Ages Past" (Isaac Watts, 1719).

[7]Ibid., 250.

[8]Ibid., 249. King's emphasis on rediscovering the precious values of the past is in accord with the biblical prophets who often called Israel to remember the One who had brought them out of slavery and into the promised land. Unsurprisingly, King often quoted the prophets, using their words to critique people who left behind the principles of love and justice that the prophets had embraced.

absolutely proscribes hatred among humanity. "Eternally so," King preached, "absolutely so. It's *wrong* to hate. (*Yes, That's right*) It always has been wrong and it always will be wrong!"[9] In King's thought, only when we remember the divine moral laws (the principles of love, justice, and peace), as well as the God "behind the process," can we begin to act creatively in our lives and in the lives of others.[10] Without these historical principles to guide our actions, and without the God of history to support us, our lives will self-destruct, and we will find ourselves destroying the lives of others.

Somebody Helped Us

King took his own advice and intentionally sought to rediscover mighty precious values in his own past. More particularly, he frequently called to mind the values taught by the men and women who had played an important role in forming his moral character during the early years of his life. For example, King often remembered his beloved mother, Alberta Williams King, and her efforts to mold his personality in constructive ways. In particular, he would replay in his mind the time she had taken him on her knee after a sad encounter with childhood racism, held him tight in her arms, and told him the good news that he would later pass on to millions of others: "You are as good as anyone."[11] King distinctly remembered that she had instilled a sense of "somebodyness" within him at that moment, while also teaching him that every day he must confront a

---

[9]Ibid., 251–52. Though often noted for being a religious liberal, King was a firm believer in moral absolutes. Primary among the absolutes he embraced was the proscription against killing, though he fully adopted this only after the beginning of the Montgomery movement, mostly at the urging of Bayard Rustin, a pacifist from the Quaker tradition. In many ways, King's embrace of absolutes is connected with his sense that people enjoy natural rights—God-given rights—that no action may undermine at any time or in any place.

[10]Ibid., 253. It would be a mistake to argue that King's use of the word *process* can be used as evidence to suggest that he was a proponent of process theology, but there are significant parts of King's theology to suggest that he might have been inclined to accept part of process thought. In particular, King believed in "creative evolution" or "emergent evolution," an ongoing process of creation, and he had a clear sense that all the different parts of creation were inextricably connected in a web of life. For his statement on creative and emergent evolution, see King, "Examination Answers, Christian Theology for Today," *Papers*, 1: 291.

[11]King, *Autobiography*, 4.

segregated system that told him he was "nobody."[12] "She made it clear," King recalled, "that she opposed this system and that I must never allow it to make me feel inferior...At this time Mother had no idea that the little boy in her arms would years later be involved in a struggle against the system she was speaking of."[13]

King also called to mind Daddy King, Reverend Martin Luther King Sr., and his untiring efforts as a black Baptist preacher to change not only the souls of his church members but also their problematic social conditions, especially political and economic segregation. He remembered Daddy's work with the NAACP, his refusal to ride segregated buses, and his fight to equalize teachers' salaries and eliminate Jim Crow elevators in Atlanta.

One incident stood out in particular in King's memory—the time a shoe store clerk ordered Daddy King to move from the seats in the front of the store to those in the rear, where blacks were traditionally waited on. Taking young Martin's hand, Daddy refused and stormed out of the store. "I still remember," King stated years after the incident, "walking down the street beside him as he muttered, 'I don't care how long I have to live with this system, I will never accept it.'"[14] The memory of that event, as well as the event itself, proved deeply formative for King: "With this heritage," King wrote, "it is not surprising that I also learned to abhor segregation, considering it both rationally inexplicable and morally unjustifiable."[15]

King dug deeper, too, and remembered stories of the successful social ministry of his grandfather, Reverend A.D. Williams, who ministered at Ebenezer Baptist in Atlanta, the same church where Daddy King and Martin would serve as pastors. And King reserved his favorite memories for his "saintly" grandmother, Jennie Williams,

[12]For more on King's notion of somebodyness, see Garth Baker-Fletcher, *Somebodyness: Martin Luther King, Jr., and the Theory of Dignity* (Minneapolis: Fortress Press, 1993).
[13]King, *Autobiography*, 3–4.
[14]Ibid., 8.
[15]Ibid., 5. For more on the direct ways in which Daddy King's politics fed the political ethics of King Jr., see Michael G. Long, *Against Us, But for Us: Martin Luther King, Jr., and the State* (Macon, Ga.: Mercer University Press, 2002), 7–11. See also Martin Luther King Sr. with Clayton Riley, *Daddy King: An Autobiography* (New York: William Morrow, 1980).

and the deep love he felt from her. In King's cherished memory, he was her favorite grandchild.[16]

King took that love from his grandmother, indeed from his whole family, and allowed it to shape his own worldview, especially his spiritual perspective on life. In fact, King stated that he found it "quite easy" to believe in God as love "because I grew up in a family where love was central and where lovely relationships were ever present." He found it easy to believe in the universe as "basically friendly mainly because of my uplifting hereditary and environmental circumstances," and he found it equally easy to lean toward an optimistic view of human nature because of his positive childhood experiences.[17]

When he remembered the important individuals of his past, King fully recognized that he did not pull himself up by his own bootstraps. He was "somebody" exactly because he had come from "somebodies"—saints who had taught him, in word and deed, about personal dignity, social responsibility, the love of God, the possibilities of human nature, and the need to confront evil.[18] King acknowledged that he was a civil rights leader of international import, but he also never forgot that he was the son and grandson of people who had loved him long before fame ever came his way and who had molded him into the person he had become.

King's deliberate efforts to remember the saints revealed his strong belief that we are who we are because of other people and the events of history—in King's view, there are no lone rangers in life. He emphasized this point most explicitly when speaking on the vice of self-centeredness. "You conquer self-centeredness," he preached, "by coming to the point of seeing that you are where you are today because somebody helped you to get there."[19]

---

[16]King, "An Autobiography of Religious Development," *Papers*, 1: 359.
[17]Ibid., 360. Part of what King is saying here is that his family life prepared him to accept the more theologically developed viewpoints set forth by the social gospel tradition he learned especially through Benjamin Mays, the president of Morehouse College during King's college years, and the Protestant liberal George Davis, King's major professor at Crozer Theological Seminary in Chester, Pennsylvania.
[18]I do not intend for my use of the word saints here to reflect the traditional meaning attributed to it by the Roman Catholic Church. I simply mean to refer to the good people of King's past, and I feel free to use the word because, as noted in the text, King described Jennie Williams as "saintly."
[19]King, "Conquering Self-Centeredness," *Papers*, 4: 254.

Creative living thus means recognizing that we have a past full of people who have helped us along the way. And it means calling to mind the saints so that we can realize our interconnectedness with and indebtedness to others, express our gratitude for their support, and remain humble about our own importance. If we fail to remember the saints who gave us life, in King's view, we lose our foundations and become subject to destructive egotism and delusions of grandeur. Moreover, we leave behind all the precious wisdom and values that the saints have to offer—the substantive guidance we need for creative living today and tomorrow.

So, rather than running from the past, we would do well to make the past come alive by remembering and honoring, in our own words and deeds, the critical role played by those who formed our character. The lives of the saints are not relics for us to store away, never to see again, but precious resources for creative living: They hold so much of the wisdom required for our march toward the beloved community.

Again, Never Alone

Clearly, however, King wanted us not to stop with the saints when mining the goodness found in our past, but rather to move from the saints to ourselves, rediscovering our own grace-filled stories. King himself returned time and again to personal stories in which he was the protagonist, especially when he was feeling weary from the demands of the civil rights movement. For example, when feeling a weariness wash over him because of death threats and blackmail attempts, or when he became exhausted because of lengthy negotiations with few results, King would return to the vivid memory of his kitchen encounter with the Spirit of Jesus. As he would reflect on that moment, he would once again hear Jesus call him, as if for the first time, to stand up for righteousness, to stand up for justice, to stand up for truth. Once again, as if for the first time, he would hear Jesus assure him that he would never be alone in his creative efforts to build the beloved community.

And I say it to you out of experience this morning: yes, I've seen the lightning flash. (*Yes, sir*) I've heard the thunder roll. (*Yes*) I've felt sin-breakers dashing, trying to conquer my soul. But I heard the voice of Jesus, saying still to fight on.

He promised never to leave me, (*Yes, sir*) never to leave me
alone. (*Thank you, Jesus*) No, never alone. No, never alone.
He promised never to leave me. Never to leave me alone.
(*Glory to God*)[20]

King offered this particular reflection in a sermon during the
last year of his life, 1968, more than ten years after the initial
experience, because he believed that the Spirit he had met in years
gone by could still help him move into a brighter tomorrow. Trusting
that God *was*, then, King said yes to his personal past and mined it
for strength and wisdom for, among other things, confronting present
evil. The past, as King used it, became the necessary means for
marching toward the beloved community.

Return to Our Roots

King adopted the same tactic when looking at the history of
the social communities he belonged to; beyond his own personal
life, that is, he turned to the goodness of society past as another
positive resource for marching toward the beloved community. When
he looked at U.S. society, for example, King made it a point to
rediscover the positive values expressed so eloquently in historic
documents such as the Declaration of Independence, the
Constitution, and the Bill of Rights. King then used these historic
values (freedom, for example) to criticize present actions (segregation,
for example) and point the way to a more positive future.[21] As a
master of internal criticism, King did not call for the U.S. government
to do something entirely new, but he did call upon it to return to its

[20]Martin Luther King Jr., "Unfulfilled Dreams," *A Knock at Midnight: Inspiration
from the Great Sermons of Reverend Martin Luther King, Jr.*, ed. Clayborne Carson and
Peter Holloran (New York: Warner Books, 1998), 199.

[21]Martin Marty, "Martin Luther King's Inner Spiritual Church," *Christian
Century* 2 (January 21, 1987): 44, has described this double move as a combination
of conservatism and radicalism: "Like the prophets of old, [King] would remind the
nation of its tradition, and then turn radical by confronting us with the power
latent in it." Because it notes the conservative and radical dimension in internal
criticism, Marty's words seem more fitting than Richard Lischer's in *The Preacher
King: Martin Luther King, Jr., and the Word That Moved America* (New York: Oxford
University Press, 1995), 178: "Like many of the biblical prophets who exhorted
Israel to *return* to the provisions of the covenant, the early and mid-career King
fulfilled a conservative function, for his imaginative vision of what America would
become was derived from his vision of what America had once been."

own past, when it delivered "the promise that all men, yes, black men as well as white men, would be guaranteed the unalienable rights of life, liberty, and the pursuit of happiness."[22]

King offered similar internal criticism of the Christian church.[23] When pushing forward with his campaign for civil rights, for example, he faced some of his most vicious resistance from the white church; but rather than lobbing stones from outside the church structure, he went deep within its history and called upon it to return to its roots. "There was a time," King wrote, "when the Church was very powerful—in the time when the early Christians rejoiced at being deemed worthy to suffer for what they believed."[24] In its history the church was not a status quo institution but a faithful movement of a small number of Christians intent on changing society into the inclusive reign of God. "By their effort and example," King stated, "they brought an end to such ancient evils as infanticide and gladiatorial contests."

King then moved from this history lesson to a critique of the present church. "Things are different now," he stated. "Now the

---

[22]Martin Luther King Jr., "I Have a Dream," in *A Testament of Hope: The Essential Writings of Martin Luther King, Jr.*, ed. James M. Washington, (San Francisco: Harper SanFrancisco, 1986), 217. King's appeal to the founding documents of the U.S., especially the Constitution, was not novel in the African American community. See Donald G. Nieman, *Promises to Keep: African-Americans and the Constitutional Order, 1776 to the Present* (New York: Oxford University Press, 1991). King later came to note that the founding documents were skewed in favor of white male property owners. For more on King and the Constitution, see "King, the Constitution, and the Courts: Remaining Awake Through a Great Revolution," in Lewis V. Baldwin with Rufus Burrow Jr., Barbara A. Holems, and Susan Winfield, *The Legacy of Martin Luther King, Jr.: The Boundaries of Law, Politics, and Religion* (Notre Dame, Ind.: University of Notre Dame Press, 2002), 173–211. King's appeal to the founding documents raises the interesting subject of civil religion—a topic addressed in King literature. For discussion of the ways in which King does not adopt the type of civil religion defined by Robert Bellah, see Thomas Poole, "Black Religion and Civil Religion: African-American Voices in America's 'Third Time of Trial,'" *Journal of Theology for South Africa* 77 (December 1991): 27–40. And for an excellent discussion of King and Southern civil religion, see Lewis V. Baldwin, "To Witness in Dixie," in *The Legacy of Martin Luther King, Jr.*, 1–76.

[23]Because he firmly believed in the practice of internal criticism, King discouraged frustrated Christians from leaving their churches. "You can always help a situation more," he advised, "when you are in it than you can from the outside. Internal criticism is always more effective than external criticism" ("Advice for Living," *Papers*, 4: 356).

[24]King, *Autobiography*, 200–201.

church is weak, ineffectual, content with its silent—and often even vocal—sanction of things as they are." King's message to the white Christian church was as simple as his message to the U.S. government—return to your roots and be faithful to the values expressed at your beginnings.[25]

Bogged Down by the Glory of Yesterday

For King, then, creative living requires mining the goodness of the past, ours and others', as a critical resource for today and tomorrow—for personal strength, for creative thought and action in the march toward the beloved community, and for internal criticisms of present social institutions and practices. Each of these uses of past goodness suggests that King wanted the past to be a *living* past. Indeed, he emphasized that past goodness is not for losing ourselves in but for pulling along as we move into the present and future—a point he noted especially when reflecting on the need for the Montgomery community to remain vigilant in its civil rights work after the community's early success with bus desegregation. Warning against self-satisfaction, King observed: "You can talk about what happened in the past and get bogged down by the glory of your great yesterday and fail to see the challenges of tomorrow."[26]

For King, failing to see the challenges of tomorrow is antithetical to creative living—it is living as if we are bogged down, stuck, stagnant. If we want to live creatively, we should not dwell on the glories of yesterday, but keep our eyes on the prize as we move, today and tomorrow, toward the beloved community.

More than Glory Days

Moreover, King also emphasized that the so-called glory days of the past were more than just glorious. King's own experiential

---

[25]Ibid., 201. Stanley Hauerwas characterizes King's work this way: "The issue was not justice, but memory. The crucial question remains whether Americans can ever acknowledge what it means to be a slave nation. That is what Martin Luther King Jr. never forgot and what we who follow him must remember," in "Remembering Martin Luther King Jr., Remembering," *Journal of Religious Ethics* 23 (Spring 1995), 147. But Hauerwas's main point is that King remembered his identity as a Christian: "Martin Luther King Jr. remembered his people, his savior, and his church, and he called the rest of us to share those memories. Therein lay his strength" (135).

[26]King, "Interview by Mike Wallace," *Papers*, 4: 439.

theology would not allow for a selective retrieval of the past that focused only on the good. The past, as he understood it theologically, consisted of not only God and the saints, but also evildoers, including vicious racists intent on undermining divine love and justice: Though God was in the past, the past was not God.

Rather than dismissing past struggles as if they did not exist, King committed them to memory. He recalled the day when he was no longer permitted to play with his childhood friend, a white boy whose father had put an end to the friendship. "I never will forget," King said, "what a great shock this was to me."[27] He recounted the time when he was eight years old and a white woman slapped him on the face in a downtown store, saying: "You are that nigger that stepped on my foot."[28] And he remembered the little boys and girls on his block who experienced sheer poverty. "I could never get out of my mind," King wrote, "the economic insecurity of many of my playmates and the tragic poverty of those living around me."[29]

For King, memories of difficult experiences are important to keep fresh in mind because they can provide substantive examples of the way life should not be. King understood the segregated world of his childhood to be the perfect example of what he did *not* want his own children to grow up in, and he used this memory of segregation constructively by allowing it to drive him toward counter-dreams, as well as counter-acts of love and justice.

Remembering the time the white bus driver ordered him to surrender his seat after the oratorical contest helped King dream of and work toward the day when buses would be fully integrated. Remembering the end of his childhood friendship helped him dream of and work toward the day when little black boys and girls would be able to play freely with little white girls and boys. Remembering the time he was slapped by the white woman helped him dream of and work toward the day when all blacks would at long last stand up and cry out, "We're not going to take it anymore!" And remembering

---

[27]King, "Autobiography of Religious Development," *Papers*, 1: 362.

[28]King, *Autobiography*, 9.

[29]Ibid., 10. Gerald Early, "Martin Luther King and the Middle Way," *Christian Century* 113 (August 28, 1996): 816, is wrong to claim that King's childhood, privileged because of his father's position, was not a significant influence on his growth as a social radical. I argue that King's anti-capitalist sentiment, as expressed during graduate school and later, is deeply rooted in his childhood experiences of the poverty that surrounded him in his neighborhood.

the sight of his poor playmates helped him dream of and work toward the day when no black person would ever be denied fair employment and fair wages because of the color of his or her skin.

For King, then, difficult experiences of our past are not for running away from but for keeping fresh in mind so that we can draw from them to create their opposite—a life of love and justice. In fact, King drew from both dimensions of his past, positive and negative, when forming the creative substance of his dreams and actions. On the one hand, his dream of the beloved community—an integrated society where peace and justice reign supreme—is deeply rooted in the values he had learned in the positive experiences of his past, especially those within his family, church, and schools. On the other hand, the dream is also deeply rooted in his negative experiences, which he used as fuel for moving to acts of love and justice. King knew what the dream should not include because of what he had experienced as a nightmare in his own past.

Reinterpret Our Past

King believed that a fresh memory of negative experiences is also extremely helpful for remaining realistic about our chances for making our dreams come alive. In his view, the negative experiences of our past can and should help us be realistic about the success of our work, as well as our expectations of others.

King himself was a realist of realists. He often noted that, because past history is full of examples of oppressors desperately holding onto power, the struggle for civil rights would be a protracted battle, and that freedom would have to be seized. "History," he observed, "is the long story of the fact (*Yes*) that privileged groups seldom give up their privileges without strong resistance, and they seldom do it voluntarily."[30]

The creative challenge while on the march to freedom, as he saw it, is to avoid the temptation to act out of the bitterness and hatred that can emerge from a painful past. For King, the problem

---

[30]King, "The American Dream," *Knock*, 96. If King sounds Marxist here, it is because he was. Though critical of Marx's materialism, King appreciated Marx's concern for the poor, as well as his realistic acknowledgment of the intransigence of the owners of production. Again, see Adam Fairclough, "Was Martin Luther King a Marxist?" *History Workshop* 15 (Spring 1983).

with bitterness and hatred is that they can eat away at our souls and lead us to do nothing creative for the beloved community. Dwelling, we wallow.[31]

When he looked back on his own childhood, King recognized that the negative experiences of segregation "did something to my growing personality." He recalled that, shortly after his parents explained the "race problem," just after his childhood friend could no longer play with him, "I was greatly shocked, and from that moment on I was determined to hate every white person. As I grew older and older this feeling continued to grow."[32] King was not always the King of love.[33]

King grew out of his deep sense of hatred in two ways. First, he opened his past for reinterpretation. King's parents had clearly taught him as a child that he should not hate white people and that it was

---

[31]King emphasized this point, though not in direct relation to the issue of the past, when a reader of his advice column asked how he and his wife, both of them black, could prevent their children from growing up to hate white people because of the system of segregation. King's answer focused on the destructive effects of hatred:

> You should teach your children at an early age that it is both morally wrong and psychologically harmful to hate anyone. Hate does more harm to the hater than it does to the hated. You must stress the fact that the hate and injustice, which have been heaped upon Negroes for many years, should be met with love and goodwill. Through such wholesome love on the part of Negroes it will be possible to solve the race problem much more speedily and create a society in which all men may live together as brothers. (King, "Advice for Living," *Papers*, 4: 267–68)

King offered similar advice on bitterness. When asked by a black U.S. soldier how he, the soldier, could justify fighting for a democracy that treated him like a second-class citizen, King offered a reply that included the following: "I would urge you not to become bitter. If you respond to the present situation that you confront in Alabama with bitterness, the new order which is emerging in America will be nothing but a duplication of the old order," in King, "Advice for Living," *Papers*, 4: 268. The notion of new order and old order will be discussed in the text's sections on the present moment.

[32]King, "Autobiography of Religious Development," *Papers*, 1:362.

[33]The point here is one of remarkable evolution, and we should not underestimate its significance. The young King, as portrayed by King himself, was not unlike the early Malcolm X: Both despised the white race. As I will note in the text, only when he entered college did King begin to embrace the notion that he should actually love whites, including those who treated him as if he was a "nobody." This point, I believe, expands the thesis set forth by James Cone in *Martin & Malcolm & America* (Maryknoll, N.Y.: Orbis Books, 1991). Not only did King and Malcolm grow toward each other at the end of their lives, after having been miles apart in

his Christian duty to love whites; but these lessons, however forcefully presented, did not really begin to take root until later, during his student years at Morehouse, when he began to experience whites who did not appear intent on supporting the vicious system of segregation. "I had been ready to resent the whole race," he recalled, "but as I got to see more of white people, my resentment was softened, and a spirit of cooperation took its place."[34]

King thus used his present experiences to question his difficult memories—not the substance of past events as much as their interpretation. In order to do that, he first had to *open* his past memories for reinterpretation. More exactly, he had to open his memories of encountering vicious racism, and he did exactly that—he reinterpreted the incidents as acts carried out by vicious racists, not by the whole white race.

For King, then, the painful past is not for us to isolate and then obsess on, but to place in open dialogue with present and future events: The past does not exist unto itself, but only in relation to the present and future. When King understood his own painful past in

---

thought and action; their young lives also started out together in the sense that both Malcolm and Martin despised whites. The point is also important for understanding the role of the *affections* in King's social thought and practices. I disagree with Adam Fairclough, who argues that, "Until 1965, King's radicalism was more intellectual than emotional," in "Was Martin Luther King a Marxist?" 120. Contrary to Fairclough, I maintain that there were two strong emotions that fueled King's thought on matters of race: the hatred he felt for whites while he was growing up, and the love he felt from parents who called him to follow "the more excellent way" when addressing race. King's radicalism at any point in his life is unintelligible to us unless we account for both of these emotions. Finally, on a related note, I believe that close attention to the early King—the young boy who hated whites, the graduate student who called for the demise of American capitalism, and the young minister in Montgomery who used prophetic rage to condemn America—should at least qualify the thesis in King studies that King became truly radical only in the last three years of his life. For more on the radicalization thesis, see Cone, *Malcolm & Martin & America;* Frederick L. Downing, *To See the Promised Land: The Faith Pilgrimage of Martin Luther King, Jr.* (Macon, Ga.: Mercer University Press, 1986); Adam Fairclough, *Martin Luther King, Jr.* (Athens: University of Georgia Press, 1990); Vincent Harding, *Martin Luther King: The Inconvenient Hero* (Maryknoll, N.Y.: Orbis Books, 1996); Richard Lischer, *The Preacher King;* and Kenneth Smith, "The Radicalization of Martin Luther King, Jr.: The Last Three Years," *Journal of Ecumenical Studies* 26, no. 2 (Spring 1989): 270–88.
[34]King, *Autobiography*, 14.

this creative way, he freed himself to move away from sheer hatred to a relatively cooperative spirit while dealing with certain whites.[35]

Forgive

Second, King countered the destructiveness of hatred by practicing forgiveness. He never once suggested that we should dismiss memories of a difficult past perpetrated by others, but he adamantly insisted that we should do everything in our power to prevent such memories from obstructing an experience of reconciliation that awaits us today and tomorrow. To be sure, we should recall the evil, but only with the intention of practicing forgiveness.

> Forgiveness does not mean ignoring what has been done or putting a false label on an evil act. It means, rather, that the evil act no longer remains as a barrier to the relationship. Forgiveness is a catalyst creating the atmosphere necessary for a fresh start and a new beginning. It is the lifting of a burden or the cancelling of a debt. The words "I forgive you, but I'll never forget what you've done" never explain the real nature of forgiveness. Certainly one can never forget, if that means erasing it totally from his mind. But when we forgive we forget in the sense that the evil deed is no longer a mental block impeding a new relationship.[36]

We should try not to forget past evil caused by others, then, but rather to recall the evils of the past as reasons for offering forgiveness in the present. And we should follow the same practice when we recall our own past sins. The challenge in creative living is not to ignore our past sins but to acknowledge them and place them within the practice of forgiveness.

---

[35]Of course, he also found plenty of vicious experiences in the present that wholly confirmed the reality of past pain. For example, Alabama Governor George Wallace confirmed the truth of King's memory of the white woman who had slapped him, and Birmingham Police Chief Bull Connor confirmed the truth of King's memory of the racist bus driver. In this sense, the past, in open dialogue with the present, drove him all the more to be realistic about the intransigence of racism and the resources required for wrestling power away from oppressors.

[36]Martin Luther King Jr., "Loving Your Enemies," *Strength to Love* (Philadelphia: Fortress Press, 1981), 48–49.

King's advice on the practice of self-forgiveness emerged several times in the advice column he wrote for *Ebony*. Once, when addressing a man struggling with a past in which he had fathered a child out of wedlock, King advised the young man to admit his mistake, seek forgiveness, and then turn his vision to the future. "You must not become so morbidly absorbed in a past mistake but you must seek to outlive it by creative living in the future."[37] King had no time for the self-pity that arises in someone who dwells on past mistakes, but he had all the time in the world for the creative experience of forgiveness.

Beyond Yesterday

King's focus on forgiveness reveals yet again that, though he used the past so creatively and in so many different ways, he recognized that ultimately the past is no place for dwelling. King did not attempt to leave the past behind, with the hope of losing himself in the present and future; nor did he seek to dwell in the past, ever fearful of what the present and future might bring. Instead of leaving the past behind or dwelling in it, King fully entered the past, understanding it to be both friend and enemy, and he accepted it, not as the totality of his life, but as an indispensable part of his temporal journey toward the beloved community.

Refusing to accept it as the totality of life, King understood the past to be only part of the creative life. To live creatively, in his view, is to make the past into a *living* past that can serve the beloved community today and tomorrow. As we keep the past fresh in mind, then, we must keep on keeping on.

---

[37]King, "Advice for Living," *Papers*, 4: 417. King offered similar advice at other times during his brief stint as a columnist. For example, when questioned by a troubled young woman who had given birth to a child before marrying, King stated the following:

> You must somehow turn your vision toward the future rather than the past. You should concentrate on the heights which you are determined to reach, not look back into the depths in which you once fell. With this wholesome attitude you will be able to stand up amid all of the criticisms that persons in your town will direct toward you. In other words, you can so outlive your past mistake that even the most ardent critic will develop a warm respect for you. (King, "Advice for Living," *Papers*, 4: 375)

Believe in the Future

Though he turned to the past for strength and wisdom, King clearly believed that creative living is future-oriented: It moves from the past and points itself toward the future dawning of the beloved community. If we are to live creatively, then, we must ultimately turn toward tomorrow and face the rising sun.

Intellectually, King knew that the future would come: Today always turns into tomorrow, and tomorrow always turns into the next day. For King, though, the future is not just for intellectually grasping—it is for *believing* in. "I believe in the future," he said, "because I believe in God."[38] King recognized that not everyone joined him in making this radical faith statement. "In a generation of so many colossal disappointments," he said, "men have lost faith in God, faith in man, and faith in the future. Many feel as did William Wilberforce, who in 1801 said, 'I dare not marry—the future is so unsettled.'"[39]

King took issue with those who face the future with fear and despair, and he preached time and again that, though the future may seem unsettled, it is far from it.

"I'm not worried about the future," he said. "Somewhere I read, 'The earth is the Lord's and the fulness thereof,' and I'm going on because I have faith in him. I do not know what the future holds, but I do know who holds the future. And if he'll guide us and hold our hand, we'll go on in."[40]

For King, then, God not only *was*—God *will be*. Yes, God was our help in ages past, but God is also our hope for years to come, and our eternal home, and exactly because God is in the future holding it up for us, there is no reason for us to fear it at all.[41] The future is not for fearing but is for entering into boldly.

God Has a Great Plan

The challenge of creative living, in this sense, is to step into the future, expecting great things to happen. The future, after all, is the time when God's plan for this world will come to fruition: "God has

---

[38]King, "Some Things We Must Do," *Papers,* 4: 330.
[39]King, "A Knock at Midnight," *Knock*, 69.
[40]King, "The Three Dimensions of a Complete Life," *Knock*, 135–36.
[41]King, "Rediscovering Lost Values," *Papers*, 2: 255.

a great plan for this world," King preached. "His purpose is to achieve a world where all men live together as brothers, and where every man recognizes the dignity and worth of all human personality."[42]

The purpose of God for this world is nothing less than the establishment of the beloved community, where integration, peace, and economic justice will reign. We may not always see the plan as clearly as we would like to, but let us not fear—the plan will happen. Because God—and God alone—controls the ultimate destiny of the universe, as the first chapter noted, evil will not triumph, Good Friday will not last, and the glow of Easter morning will appear on the horizon.[43] "Often love is crucified and buried in a grave," King said, "but in the long run it rises up and redeems even that which crucifies it."[44] Created by the God of the future, the arc of the universe always tilts toward justice, and so the end of life will most definitely be a social order with peace and justice.[45] We must thus keep the faith, holding despair at bay, and being ever hopeful, ever optimistic, ever positive, ever trusting that God will make a way out of no way. Creative living, in King's view, is hopeful believing that the dawn will come.

Human Progress Is Not Automatic

But, as we rightly believe that God ultimately controls the destiny of the universe, we must not just sit back and wait for the future of God to reach fulfillment here by itself. The future of God is for *us* to inaugurate. It will not arrive on its own but only through the dizzying dreams and vigorous actions of the people of God.

It is "dangerous optimism" to believe that the future of God will just roll in on its own one day out there.[46] "Such an attitude," King wrote, "stems from a tragic misconception of time, from the strangely irrational notion that there is something within the very flow of time that will inevitably cure all ills." But that is simply not

---

[42]Martin Luther King Jr., "The Death of Evil Upon the Seashore," *Birth of a New Age, December 1955–December 1956*, vol.3 of *The Papers of Martin Luther King, Jr.*, ed. Clayborne Carson et al.(Berkeley: University of California Press, 1992), 261–62.

[43]Ibid., 259.

[44]King, "Advice for Living," *Papers*, 4: 306.

[45]King, "Address to MIA Mass Meeting at Holt Street Baptist Church," *Papers*, 3: 200.

[46]King, "Facing the Challenge of a New Age," *Papers*, 3: 460.

the case: "Human progress never rolls in on wheels of inevitability; it comes through the tireless efforts of men willing to be co-creators with God, and without this hard work, time itself becomes an ally of the forces of social stagnation."[47]

Though inevitable, the glorious future of God is not magical: It needs *us* to pull it into the present. *We* need to speed up tomorrow by making it today. Yes, God has a plan that will be fulfilled, but a key part of the divine plan is for us, with the help of God, to bring the plan to fulfillment. In this sense, the future is ours to create.

This Is a Great Dream

For King, creating the future requires the practice of dreaming, and not just any dream will do.[48] When King envisioned the future, he dreamed of God's hope for this world—the time when the lion and the lamb would lie down together, when little boys and girls would be judged not by the color of their skin but by the content of their character, and when justice would roll down like waters and righteousness like an ever-flowing stream. King found social expression of the divine plan in what he labeled "the American dream," a theme he addressed in a sermon on Independence Day in 1965:

> It wouldn't take us long to discover the substance of that dream. It is found in those majestic words of the Declaration of Independence, words lifted to cosmic proportions: "We hold these truths to be self-evident, that all men are created equal, that they are endowed by [their] Creator with certain inalienable Rights, that among these are Life, Liberty, and the pursuit of Happiness." This is a dream. It's a great dream.[49]

In King's view, what made the dream so great was its embracing of both universalism ("It doesn't say 'some men,' it says 'all men'")

[47]King, *Autobiography*, 196.

[48]King's classic statement on his dreams, of course, is found in the "I Have a Dream" speech he delivered during the March on Washington in 1963. For an excellent description of the context and content of this speech, see Patrick Henry Bass, *Like a Mighty Stream: The March on Washington—August 28, 1963* (Philadelphia: Running Press, 2002).

[49]King, "The American Dream," *Knock*, 86.

and God-given rights that each individual enjoys and that no government may rightly take away.[50] "The American dream reminds us, and we should think about it anew on this Independence Day," King preached, "that every man is an heir of the legacy of dignity and worth."[51]

King believed that the American dream's embrace of the dignity and worth of each person, as well as the interconnectedness of all humanity, is directly traceable to the biblical concept of the *imago Dei*.

> You see, the founding fathers were really influenced by the Bible. The whole concept of the *imago dei*, as it is expressed in Latin, the "image of God," is the idea that all men have something within them that God injected. Not that they have substantial unity with God, but that every man has a capacity to have fellowship with God. And this gives him a uniqueness, it gives him worth, it gives him dignity. And we must never forget this as a nation: There are no gradations in the image of God. Every man from a treble white to a bass black is significant on God's keyboard, precisely because every man is made in the image of God. One day we will learn that. (*Yes*) We will know one day that God made us to live together as brothers and to respect the dignity and worth of every man.[52]

In King's view, based on his theological understanding of the image of God, this is exactly what the substance of our dream should be—the vision of a time when everyone honors each individual as possessing dignity and worth, and when all individuals live together

---

[50] Ibid.

[51] Ibid., 86–87.

[52] Ibid., 88. King frequently cited both the Bible and the founding documents of the U.S. at the same time. He found their themes to be overlapping and refused to believe that good Christians could not also be good patriots. Of course, King's patriotism was a theologically principled patriotism; he loved his country because he believed that its purpose, as stated in the founding documents, coincided with the will of God.

as brothers and sisters.[53] In more concrete terms, King believed that this time would arrive when the world experiences integration, peace, and economic justice, and so these conditions, physical and spiritual in character, should also be the concrete stuff of our dream.

More fundamentally, King believed that this is what the future is for—dreaming in bright and bold colors. King held that because God is in the future, we have countless reasons to dream of the day when the beloved community will debut in history, and because God is able to transform the midnight of the world into the dawn from on high, we have an abiding responsibility as part of the people of God to dream of that dawn even and especially when the midnight of life surrounds us.[54] And let us make no mistake about it—the midnight of life does surround our efforts to act on the American dream. Because of the abiding presence of the three challenges to the American dream—segregation, militarism, and economic injustice—King conceded that the dream, God's plan for the world, often shatters.

Unfulfilled Dreams

In King's own life, the American dream was often shattered. For example, when four little girls were killed by a bomb that ripped through their Birmingham church shortly after the March on Washington, King felt, perhaps most deeply in his life, that the dream of the fulfillment of God's plan had turned downright nightmarish.

Near the end of his life, having suffered nightmare after nightmare, King observed that "unfulfilled dreams" are simply a part

---

[53]It is not possible to overemphasize the significance of "the image of God" in King's theology. Its significance is found especially in King's reply to a reader of the advice column who asked him whether a Christian could also be a segregationist. "I do not feel," King wrote, "that a man can be a Christian and a staunch segregationist simultaneously. All men, created alike in the image of God, are inseparately bound together. This is at the very heart of the Christian Gospel. This broad universalism standing at the center of the Christian Gospel makes segregation morally evil." King, "Advice for Living," *Papers*, 4: 281.

[54]King emphasized the theme of dawn and darkness frequently throughout his life. Here is another beautiful example of that use: "God has the light that can shine through all the darkness. We have experiences when the light of day vanishes, leaving us in some dark and desolate midnight—moments when our highest hopes are turned into the shambles of despair…But ever and again, we look toward the east and discover that there is another light which shines even in the darkness" (King, *Autobiography*, 128).

of creative living. "So many of us in life," he preached, "start out building temples: temples of character, temples of justice, temples of peace. And so often we don't finish them." We don't finish them because we cannot. "And I guess one of the great agonies of life is that we are constantly trying to finish that which is unfinishable. We are commanded to do that."[55] Consider David's dream of building the temple of the Lord, the apostle Paul's dream of preaching in Spain, Woodrow Wilson's dream of a successful League of Nations, and Gandhi's dream of unity in India: Shattered dreams are the stuff of life.

In the face of shattered dreams, King's advice was clear: Do not stop dreaming. Instead, we must wake up, turn over, and dream again, but this time being realistic that the big dreams may not reach their fulfillment as soon as we would like them to. King did exactly that, adjusting both the timetable and the content of his dreams. For example, when asked whether his goal of integration was achievable in his lifetime, he confessed his belief that present and future racism would prevent the dream from becoming real overnight. With human sin in mind, he also fought for integration first by seeking desegregation, a negative condition that was merely foundational for the more positive step of integration.

Yes, the man of the future was wary of the future. As long as King had experienced it, the future never once proved to be the perfect embodiment of the will of God: Tomorrow had always brought problems, and sometimes they seemed even worse than yesterday's. For example, when the little girls were bombed in 1963, life seemed much worse than it had in 1955, when Rosa Parks was merely arrested for not surrendering her seat to a white passenger.

King knew that, because the future holds not only God but also a sinful humanity, the future would always bring its own imperfections. Sin and evil would not magically disappear in the future, and given their ongoing presence, we would do well to avoid expecting that our earthy future can mirror our heavenly future. An imperfect earth will never become a perfect heaven.

Still Dreaming

Still, no matter how many blows he and the movement suffered, no matter how many nightmares visited him during the course of

---

[55]King, "Unfulfilled Dreams," *Knock*, 192.

one night, King kept on dreaming: He kept hope alive.[56] Hope, in King's ethic, "is a final refusal to give up...It means going on *anyhow*."[57] So when he confessed his belief that the beloved community was not just around the corner, he also said, "But [that day] is certainly my hope and dream. Indeed, it is the keystone of my faith in the future that we will someday be a thoroughly integrated society."[58] Even when he looked back on the nightmares that followed the March on Washington, King proclaimed his abiding belief that the future would indeed bring a brighter tomorrow—a day when the American dream would be fulfilled. King's 1965 statement of faith is worth quoting at length:

> So yes, the dream has been shattered, (*Amen*) and I have had my nightmarish experiences, but I tell you this morning once more that I haven't lost the faith. (*No, sir*) I still have a dream (*A dream. Yes, sir*) that one day all of God's children will have food and clothing and material well-being for their bodies, culture and education for their minds, and freedom for their spirits. (*Yes*)
>
> I still have a dream this morning: (*Yes*) One day all of God's black children will be respected like his white children.
>
> I still have a dream this morning (*Yes*) that one day the lion and the lamb will lie down together, and every man will sit under his own vine and fig tree and none shall be afraid.
>
> I still have a dream this morning that one day all men everywhere will recognize that out of one blood God made all men to dwell upon the face of the earth.

---

[56]After I wrote this sentence, I read, and completely agreed with, James H. Cone, "Martin Luther King, Jr., and the Third World," *Journal of American History* 74, no. 2 (September 1987), 467: "No matter how difficult the struggle for justice became, no matter how powerful were the opponents of justice, no matter how many people turned against him, King refused absolutely to lose hope, because he believed that ultimately right will triumph over wrong." On a related note, Adam Fairclough, in *Martin Luther King, Jr.*, puts the point this way: "For all his depression, King never gave in to despair" (127).

[57]Martin Luther King Jr., "The Meaning of Hope," quoted in Robert Michael Franklin, "An Ethic of Hope: The Moral Thought of Martin Luther King, Jr.," *Union Seminary Quarterly Review* 40 (January 1986): 49.

[58]King, "*Playboy* Interview 1965," *Testament*, 375.

I still have a dream this morning (*Yes, sir*) that one day every valley shall be exalted, and every mountain and hill will be made low; the rough places will be made plain, and the crooked places straight; and the glory of the Lord shall be revealed, and all flesh shall see it together.

I still have a dream this morning (*Amen*) that truth will reign supreme and all of God's children will respect the dignity and worth of human personality. And when this day comes the morning stars will sing together (*Yes*) and the sons of God will shout for joy.

"We hold these truths to be self-evident, that all men (*All right*) are created equal, that they are endowed by their Creator with certain inalienable Rights, (*Yes, sir*) that among these are Life, Liberty, and the pursuit of Happiness."[59]

No Hope, No Creativity

In the final analysis, King was a prophet who embraced the virtue of hope as strongly as he held on to faith and love (*agape*). The virtue of hope was not a situational option for him, primarily because he grounded his hope not in human nature but in the character of God. "Faith in the dawn," he proclaimed, "arises from the faith that God is good and just."[60] Exactly because God is good and just, "the dawn will come. Disappointment, sorrow, and despair are born at midnight, but morning follows."[61] And exactly because God is eternal, so too is the message that morning is our destiny. "Our *eternal* message of hope," King stated repeatedly, "is that dawn will come."[62]

In addition, the virtue of hope was not a situational option for King because he understood it to be a fundamental part of creative living. "When you lose hope," he stated, "you lose creativity, you lose rationality. Hope is necessary for creativity and spirituality. Hope is one of the basic structures for an adequate life."[63]

Because he believed that God is good and just, and that hope is necessary for creative living, King never surrendered his life of hopeful

[59]King, "The American Dream," *Knock*, 99–100.
[60]King, "A Knock at Midnight," *Knock*, 76.
[61]Ibid., 78. King turns here to the witness of Psalm 30:5.
[62]Ibid., 75 (emphasis mine).
[63]King, "The Meaning of Hope," quoted in Franklin, "An Ethic of Hope," 50.

living. Even in March of 1968, just before his death, when he was
planning for the Poor People's Campaign, King announced that he
would "not yield to a politic of despair."[64] Instead, he stressed his
"ethic of hope":

> We're going to win freedom because both the sacred heritage
> of our nation and the eternal will of the Almighty God are
> embodied in our echoing demands. And so, however dark it
> is, however deep the angry feelings are, and however violent
> explosions are, I can still sing "We Shall Overcome."[65]

Time for Action

But, again, it is through *our* actions that God can and will make
a way out of no way. The future, then, is not only to be dreamed—
it is also to be fought for. The future is for us to inaugurate by
allowing God to empower us to carry out the most vigorous of
actions in support of the American dream. King would often say
that the movement had come a long way but that it also had a long,
long way to go.[66] This realistic assessment led him to one conclusion:
Now is the time for action. The future is for enacting right here and
right now, and the time has come for us to speed up our destiny. In
this sense, King understood the future not as a distant possibility but
as the substance for our actions today: *Today* we are to inaugurate
tomorrow. And King believed that we can begin to do exactly that, if
only we would trust that God has a plan that will succeed. This was
King's own conviction up to the last day of his life. Unflappably
hopeful, he always saw the future as "a path upward, not downward,"
a path we must take right now—in this present moment.[67]

---

[64]King, "Remaining Awake through a Great Revolution," *Knock*, 222.

[65]Ibid., 223. I disagree with Richard Lischer's sense that King's hope dissipated
in the last part of his life. "[King's] sermons of this period," Lischer writes, "do not
dispense with metaphorical language, but the soaring images of hope have
disappeared," in *The Preacher King*, 160. King preached hope even in his last sermon,
"I've Been to the Mountaintop," and he did so exactly because of his "ethic of
hope"—his abiding trust that God, with the help of God's people, would make a
way out of no way. For the phrase "ethic of hope," I am indebted to Robert Michael
Franklin, "An Ethic of Hope," 49–50.

[66]See, for example, Martin Luther King Jr., "A Realistic Look at the Question
of Progress in the Area of Race Relations," *Papers*, 4: 167–79.

[67]King, "A Testament of Hope," *Testament*, 314.

Now Is a Great Time to Be Alive

"If I were standing at the beginning of time, and the Almighty gave me a panoramic view of the whole of history, and then proceeded to ask me which age I would prefer to live in…" With these words King set out on a grand thought experiment that resulted in a strong embrace of the present moment. King suggested that if he were standing at the beginning of time, he would bypass the glory of Greek culture, the power of the Roman Empire, the artistry of the Renaissance, even the French and American Revolutions. Bypassing all these, he would then turn to God and say, "If you allow me to live just a few years in the second half of the 20th Century, I will be happy."

King recognized that others had found the time of his life to be "a ghastly period of our nation's history," but he disagreed, sensing that "something is happening in the world today that hasn't happened before"—a world revolution. "The drama of freedom and justice is unfolding today in a way unprecedented before. This is truly a great time to be alive."[68] Clearly, King was referring to the powerful events of the 1950s—the desegregation of the South, the de-colonization of Africa, and the new dignity felt by blacks around the world. But, more fundamentally, he was also referring to the power of the present moment—the locus of God's creative activity.

God Lives

For King, today is the day. Yes, the days of yesteryear held their share of glory, but the day of days was not way back with the Greeks, Romans, or Italians, even at their peak of peaks. Today is *the* time to be alive—living creatively—because now is when God lives. As noted in the first chapter, King would often say, "Remember. God lives!"[69] For King, God is not stuck in the past somewhere, nor has God fled

---

[68]King, "Remarks in Acceptance of the Forty-second Spingarn Medal in the Forty-eighth Annual NAACP Convention," *Papers,* 4: 230.
[69]King, "To Fred L. Shuttlesworth," *Papers*, 3: 496.

to tomorrow. Rather, God lives—God simply *is*, right here and right now, and God is here to stay.[70]

In King's view, whenever the love and justice of God rule in our lives, there *is* the reign of God. Whenever the social order advances, there *is* the reign of God. Yes, the divine reign *was* given new direction in the ministry of Jesus many years ago, but the Spirit of Jesus *is* continuously present in the love and justice we show to ourselves, others, and God, and in the love and justice that others reveal.[71] So, whatever we do, we must never abandon the present— we must enter it.

Time and Eternity

Because God is here, the present is for entering into and living in creatively. Creative living in the present moment means many things in King's view. The following three chapters will suggest that King understood creative living to mean acting for the beloved community (that is, eliminating oppression, forming moral character in the ways of Jesus, and creating social structures that reflect the love and justice of God); temporarily withdrawing from such action so that we can have time to reflect, pray, spend time with family and friends, and regain the energy we need for even more vigorous action; and even deliberately preparing ourselves for death. As foundational work for the following chapters, this section simply suggests that, for King, creative living means doing the will of God by holding a tension between time and eternity and seeking to create, even in the midst of suffering, a new world that embodies the principles of eternity.

"Every true Christian," King wrote, "is a citizen of two worlds, the world of time and eternity."[72] On the one hand, we live in the

---

[70]King, "The Three Dimensions of a Complete Life," *Knock*, 135. In a passage on God's independence, King stated:

And God is the only person in the universe that can say "I Am" and put a period behind it. Each of us sitting here has to say "I am because of my parents; I am because of certain environmental conditions; I am because of certain hereditary circumstances; I am because of God." But God is the only being that can just say "I Am" and stop right there. "I Am that I Am." And he's here to stay.

[71]King, "Qualifying Examination Answers, Theology of the Bible," *Papers*, 1: 206.

[72]King, "Transformed Nonconformists," *Strength*, 18.

colony of time, with its human institutions, laws, customs, ideas, practices, and roles. Many parts of this colony can be quite helpful for everyday living. For example, the federal judicial system in the United States is a helpful, even necessary, ingredient for regulating the everyday conduct of human affairs among U.S. citizens.

According to King, when this colony of time uplifts the human personality, it is important for us to reside in it as supportive citizens, doing all we can to buttress its goodness. At the same time, though, it is important for us to remember that the colony of time is transitory and evanescent, and that parts of it often contradict the will of God. The colony of time often contradicts the divine will exactly because it is so human, so sinful, and this means the obvious: "The kingdom of God is *not yet.* Because sin exists on every level of man's existence, the death of one tyranny is followed by the emergence of another tyranny." [73] Though God is in the present, then, the present is not God.

So, while we reside in the colony of time, we must be ever aware that we can never rightly equate it with the will of God. To avoid confusing the two, we must always remember that, though we are part of the colony of time, we are also part of a colony of heaven, an empire of eternity marked by the divine principles of love and justice.

As citizens of *this* empire, we owe our ultimate allegiance not to any human institutions, even the church, but to the eternal love of God. "Living in the colony of time," King stated, "we are ultimately responsible to the empire of eternity." Yes, we must put in our time here, but we must never conform to any "time-bound custom or earth-bound idea." [74] Eternity, that is, always trumps time. So when we face destructive time-bound customs (for example, militarism and economic injustice), we must always keep in mind that, though we are *in* the world, we are not *of* the world. Living *in* the present, we are not bound *to* the present: God frees us, right here and right now, to reside in the empire of eternity and to answer to God alone. The ever-present question thus becomes, "Will we march only to the music of time, or will we, risking criticism and abuse, march to

---

[73]King, "The Death of Evil Upon the Seashore," *Strength*, 82.
[74]King, "Transformed Nonconformist," *Strength*, 18.

the soul-saving music of eternity?"[75] For King, the challenge of creative living in the moment is to recognize the soul-saving music of eternity and to turn it up, marching the whole way, so that we can drown out the music of time.

Make a New World

King believed that right now is a great time to begin the march. The present world, as he saw it, is undergoing a dramatic transformation in focus and direction. Using only a slight variation on the theme of time and eternity, King stated that living in the present, right here and right now, is to exist within and between a dying old world and an emerging new one. More exactly, the present is home to a fundamental shift between these two worlds: The new is replacing the old.

The dying old world includes everything in the colony of time that is opposed to the beloved community—racial segregation and discrimination, economic injustice, warmongering, colonialism, and imperialism. Conversely, the emerging new world includes the eternal divine will and everything human that marks the beginning of the beloved community—love, justice, and peace.

Because the old is not yet gone, and because the new is not yet fully present, creative living in the moment entails the double response noted above. On the one hand, creative living is a matter of rejecting the old world that still exists. It is not a matter of rejecting the *people* of the old world, but it is a matter of rejecting the old world's institutions, laws, customs, ideas, practices, and roles. Anything that stands in the way of love, peace, and justice demands our present resistance. On the other hand, though, creative living is a matter of speeding the day when the new world will be here fully. In King's view, the present is pregnant with the new world—in fact, the head is already showing. And so the challenge of creative living in the moment is not just to resist the old but also to assume the role of midwife—to act as a catalyst for the birth.

As King put it, our present challenge is to "make of this old world a new world."[76] As we reject the old world, then, we should seek to create new institutions, laws, customs, ideas, practices, and

[75]Ibid., 25.
[76]King, "The Drum Major Instinct," *Knock*, 186.

roles that embody and reflect the positive values of love, peace, and justice. For example, as we reject segregated institutions, we should seek to create truly integrated ones. Or, as we resist the old world temptation to be bitter, we should allow God to create a new heart within us—a heart full of forgiveness.[77]

Cruciform Living

Of course, pulling away from the old world entails pain and suffering—which means that there can be no creative living without present suffering.[78] King conceded that the birth pangs could seem overwhelming and, at times, too much to take. Indeed, given all the death threats he faced, let alone the actual physical abuse he received, King knew all about suffering at the hands of oppressors who would not voluntarily concede power, and yet he never suggested running away from it or allowing it to consume us.

> As my sufferings mounted I soon realized that there were two ways that I could respond to my situation: either to react with bitterness or seek to transform the suffering into a creative force. I decided to follow the latter course. Recognizing the necessity for suffering, I have tried to make of it a virtue. If only to save myself from bitterness, I have attempted to see my personal ordeals as an opportunity to

---

[77]The subsequent two chapters will provide greater detail of the attitude and actions required for moving into the beloved community.

[78]King, of course, did not believe that pulling away from the old order is the only thing that causes suffering. A simple overview of his theology of suffering is actually located in a reply, in his advice column ("Advice for Living," *Papers*, 4: 280), to a reader who asked whether God makes us suffer because of our sins and the sins of our ancestors:

> You are really raising the question, "Why do men suffer?" It is often true that we suffer because of sins we consciously or unconsciously commit. There are moral laws of the universe just as abiding as the physical laws, and when we disobey these moral laws we suffer tragic consequences. It is also true that the interrelatedness of human life often necessitates our suffering for the sins of our forefathers. We must admit, however, that we are often the victims of pain and suffering that cannot be explained by sins committed by ourselves or our forefathers. We must admit that there is some mystery surrounding God's being. There are certain things that happen in our lives and in the life of the universe that we just can't explain in rational terms. You must live by the faith that all suffering has some purpose which the finite mind of man can never comprehend.

transform myself and heal the people involved in the tragic situation which now obtains. I have lived these past few years with the conviction that unearned suffering is redemptive.[79]

Behind these comments lies King's belief in the redemptive nature of the suffering of the crucified Jesus—suffering that Jesus' followers should willingly accept. Too many times Christians avoid suffering, believing that life with Jesus means comfort, happiness, and rest, but King stressed otherwise in 1966:

> We are gravely mistaken to think that religion protects us from the pain and agony of mortal existence. Life is not a euphoria of unalloyed comfort and untroubled ease. Christianity has always insisted that the cross we bear precedes the crown we wear. To be a Christian one must take up his cross, with all its difficulties and agonizing and tension-packed content, and carry it until that very cross leaves its marks upon us and redeems us to that more excellent way which comes only through suffering.[80]

Creative living is therefore cruciform living—cross-centered living: It is all about entering into present pain and suffering for the right cause, and being prepared to die for it. "The end of life is not to be happy," King said. "The end of life is not to achieve pleasure and avoid pain. The end of life is to do the will of God, *come what may*."[81] The following chapters will explore further what it means to

---

[79]King, "Suffering and Faith," *Testament*, 41.

[80]King, "Beyond Discovery, Love," Dallas, Texas, September 25, 1966, 8; quoted in David J. Garrow, "Martin Luther King, Jr., and the Spirit of Leadership," *Journal of American History* 74, no. 2 (September 1987): 438-47. See also King, *Strength to Love*, 24–25. The quote in Garrow, though, is more interesting because the *Strength* text lacks the comment on life as other than euphoria.

[81]King, "Paul's Letter to American Christians," *Papers*, 3: 419 (emphasis mine); John Ansbro, *Martin Luther King, Jr.: Nonviolent Strategies and Tactics for Social Change* (1982; reprint, Landham, Md.: Madison Books, 2000), 55, traces this statement to L. Harold DeWolf, *A Theology of the Living Church* (New York: Harper & Row, 1953; rev., 1960), 138–39. Dewolf, King's mentor at Boston University, wrote: "Whether I am today suffering pain or enjoying pleasurable health will make little difference a thousand years from now. But how my pain or pleasure, weakness or health are related to faith and love will make all the difference."

do the will of God, but here the important point is that, for King, doing the will of God, *come what may*, even the cross, is the very essence of living creatively in the moment.

Keep On Keeping On

Come what may. King's understanding of the purpose of life has part of its roots in the kitchen epiphany. Remember the overwhelming fear he faced in the early days of Montgomery, as well as his hidden desire to abandon his leadership position in light of all the threats against his life. In those moments, King allowed himself to enter the depths of his soul and to cry out in anguish— the present suffering called for nothing less.

Yet he did not simply cry out. In the kitchen experience, he let all the anguish pour out from him, but then he opened himself to the love of God still in the moment, trusting that even where unbelievable pain is present, so is God. And after the kitchen experience, King stood up and then immersed himself ever more deeply into the present work of establishing the beloved community, even though the death threats mounted day by day. At that point, the goal of his life became doing the will of God, *come what may*.

King expected the same from his followers. Yes, pain and suffering may have the present upper hand. "But we must keep on moving and keep on keeping on," he said.[82] Creative living thus endures all things, especially the pain that results from doing the will of God in the old world.

Born for the Stars

Still, King understood that the present journey to the new world is not all about suffering: Life is so much more than suffering, even redemptive suffering. As the fourth chapter will note, King saw the beauty of God within and around him, and so he sought to appreciate and enjoy life as much as he could, even in the midst of overwhelming pain. King, in other words, was no ascetic: He thoroughly enjoyed delicious Southern meals, just like the kind his mother had made. He imbibed his share of the fruit of the vine, and inhaled the rich flavor of Southern tobacco. He loved the company of friends, male

---

[82]King, "Address to MIA Mass Meeting at Holt Street Baptist Church," *Papers,* 4: 432.

and female, who let him be himself, and he reveled in his children and in the beauties of natural scenes. King even loved to dance.

But, clearly, hedonism was not his personal philosophy. Unlike those who suggest that we should eat, drink, and be merry, for tomorrow we die, he found no ultimate satisfaction in living in the moment just for the experience of pleasure. King expressed this point in reply to an *Ebony* reader who wondered if she was being "snobbish" for expressing her dissatisfaction with members of her social set who seemed to be devoted to cars, gossip, and alcohol. Taking her side, King wrote: "You are simply living by the principle that every individual is made for that which is high, noble, and good. Man is more than a dog to be satisfied by the bones of sensory pleasure and showy materialism. He is a being of spirit, born for the stars and created for eternity."[83]

Creative living in the moment thus embraces the present pleasures of God's creation, but it does not lose itself in "sensory pleasure and showy materialism." This means that creative living requires us to embrace not just any pleasure but the kind of pleasure that allows us to be true to who we are—"born for the stars and created for eternity." Such pleasure is creative pleasure; it builds up our personality by immersing us in what is "high, noble, and good" in life. And so, yes, we should enjoy the fruit of God's creation, but we must make sure along the way that our pleasurable experiences serve rather than undermine our mission to do the will of God, come what may.

For King, then, to live creatively in the moment is to immerse ourselves, right here and right now, in both the horror and beauty of God's creation, while being willing and ready at all times to die for the love of God. Creative living is living life to its fullest while at the same time preparing to die.

Coda: Creative Living in the Past, Present, and Future

Finally, King refused to understand the present to be an isolated dimension of temporal existence. King believed that we know the

---

[83]King, "Advice for Living," *Papers*, 4: 306. James Colaiaco, *Martin Luther King, Jr.: Apostle of Militant Nonviolence* (New York: St. Martin's Press, 1988), 203, has rightly argued that "The genius of Martin Luther King, Jr., was his ability to perceive that there is something noble in humanity that, once tapped, has the power to transform the world."

past only because we have a present, that we experience the present only because we have a past, and that we can hope for the future only because we have a present that our past gave birth to. Like time itself, we flow from the past, through the present, and into the future, and so creative living—marching toward the beloved community— requires nothing less than holding together the three dimensions of temporal existence.

More exactly, for King, we cannot attain the beloved community by dwelling in or deserting the past, but we can begin to march toward the community by remembering the saints who embodied love and justice and by offering and receiving forgiveness for past sins: The beloved community emerges from the practices of remembering and forgiving. Nor can we attain the beloved community by abandoning or glorifying the future, but we can begin to march toward it by dreaming of becoming everything we can be in the community: The beloved community also emerges from the practice of hoping.

We march toward the beloved community, then, when we relate to the past and future dialectically. We take a step forward when we say no to a past that would enslave us in regret, and a future that would abstract us from the realistic assessment of everyday life. We take another step forward when we say yes to a past that can teach us about the virtues of the beloved community, and a future that can empower us to move beyond the despair of the present moment.

When we relate to the past and future dialectically, we free ourselves to live, right here and right now, for the love of God. Because God is already here, there is no reason to go anywhere else—the present is the most fitting time for us to act for the beloved community. Moreover, the present moment is the only time when we can march toward the beloved community: It is only *now* when we can dream, it is only *now* when we can make our dreams come alive, and it is only *now* when we can hear God calling us to water the seeds of the community that are already here. This is why King said yes to the present, regardless of whether it brings happiness or pain and suffering.

But King said no to the present, too, mainly because he knew all too well that the beloved community is not here fully. Perfect love, justice, and peace do not exist exactly because we and others continue to exist as we are—sinful and limited.

And so, at long last, the best way to march toward the beloved community is by saying yes and no even to the present, where the love of God already *is*. Yes, we must celebrate the beginnings of the beloved community right here and right now, but we must also recognize that the true beloved community rests well beyond the present moment. It begins right now and will come to greater completion in our earthly future, but it will reach its full completion only when the God of our heavenly future wipes away all the tears.

Make a Career of Humanity
Advice for Acting

Now is the time for us to *act*. For King, it was just not good enough for us to know the will of God in time or even to testify to God in our community of faith. "You've seen these people," he railed in 1967, "who have a high blood pressure of creeds and an anemia of deeds."[1] Because faith without works is dead, our mission in life is to *do* the will of God, right here and right now, come what may. In King's view, creative living—marching toward the beloved community—is action-packed.

Hammers and Anvils

King's assertion that our primary reason for living is to *make* the will of God come alive is deeply rooted in his theological understanding of the human person. According to King's theological study of humanity, God has created us to act, not merely to be acted

---

[1]Martin Luther King Jr., "The Three Dimensions of a Complete Life," *A Knock at Midnight: Inspiration from the Great Sermons of Reverend Martin Luther King, Jr.,* ed. Clayborne Carson and Peter Holloran (New York: Warner Books, 1998), 133.

upon. God has empowered us to be makers of history, not victims of history. God has formed us into hammers, not anvils. Essentially, we are deciders and doers.[2]

King lamented what he considered to be the contemporary human tendency to avoid action—the inclination to squelch the core of our identity. "Who doubts," he asked, "that today most men are anvils and are shaped by the patterns of the majority?"[3] Allowing ourselves to be passively shaped into the image of the majority, according to King, destroys nothing less than the essence of the active individuals God has created us to be.

On a related note, one of King's firmest convictions was that we lose touch with our essence when we become fatalistic, believing that everything is foreordained and inescapable. Not only is fatalism an injustice to our essence; it is also an affront to the very character of God. "Some fatalists," King stated, "are very religious people who think of God as the determiner and controller of destiny."[4] But God is not a dictator or a puppeteer. "We must surely affirm the majesty and sovereignty of God," King proclaimed, "but this should not lead us to believe that God is an Almighty Monarch who will impose his will upon us and deprive us of the freedom to choose

---

[2]Martin Luther King Jr., "Transformed Nonconformist," *Strength to Love* (Philadelphia: Fortress Press, 1981), 19. These are just some of the images King used when emphasizing the active dimension of creative living. On the theme of human action and King, I agree with Samuel Dubois Cook: "One of King's most precious legacies was his stress on human freedom and responsibility, individual and collective. He did not believe that men are mere victims, spectators or by-standers in history, that they are powerless before the tidal sweep of inevitable forces and predetermined systems, that what men do makes no difference in the outcome. He believed, rather, that social institutions and forces are molded by human choice and effort," in "Is Martin Luther King, Jr., Irrelevant?" *New South* 26 (Spring 1971): 14.

[3]King, "Transformed Nonconformist," *Strength*, 19. As the second chapter noted, King commended the early church exactly because it stood against the majority and fought for the elimination of violence in its society. See Martin Luther King Jr., *The Autobiography of Martin Luther King, Jr.,* ed. Clayborne Carson (New York: Warner Books, 1998), 200–201.

[4]King, "Shattered Dreams," *Strength*, 89. It is important to note here that on occasion King did indeed refer to God as the controller of destiny, but by this he meant that God controls the ultimate destiny of the creation, especially as it takes form in the life hereafter. Never did King understand God as a divine being that controls the inner workings of the human heart and mind.

what is good or what is not good."[5] For King, God is a loving Parent who gives us the resources we need to decide and act for ourselves.

What Will Happen If We Don't Help?

We are able to do something because God has freed us to deliberate, decide, and act, and this is exactly what God expects of us—that we will weigh the consequences of inaction, seize our freedom, and decide and do.[6] "This," King emphasized, "is what God needs today: men and women who will ask 'What will happen to humanity if I don't help? (*Oh yeah*) What will happen to the civil rights movement if I don't participate? (*Yes*) What will happen to my city if I don't vote? (*Oh yeah*) What will happen to the sick if I don't visit them?'"[7]

For King, God is not the only creator in town; we are creators, too. Yes, God is active in history, bringing about the new age that holds the beloved community, but let us not think for a second that God intends for us to do nothing. If we think all we have to do is wait for God to solve everything, we are victims of "an illusion wrapped in superficiality."[8] Contrary to popular piety, God will *not* redeem the world in God's own good time, that is, a time magically separate from human action. In fact, without our own hard work to fill it, time will end up destroying the will of God—hence, the desperate need for us to work for the beloved community today.

But, as we work, we must beware of the countless obstructions we will encounter. When we live creatively, King believed, we will

---

[5]King, "The Answer to a Perplexing Question," *Strength*, 133. King's language here goes back to a graduate school critique he offered of Calvin's doctrine of predestination. King criticized Calvin's doctrine of predestination by arguing that responsibility and reason can exist, as they do, only because of the presence of human freedom. "Freedom," King wrote, "is both a moral and metaphysical necessity" (Martin Luther King, Jr., "A Comparison and Evaluation of the Theology of Luther with That of Calvin," *Rediscovering Precious Values, July 1951–November 1955*, vol. 2 of *The Papers of Martin Luther King, Jr.,* ed. Clayborne Carson et al. [Berkeley: University of California Press, 1994], 190–91).

[6]King defined freedom as the capacity to deliberate, decide, and respond. See Martin Luther King Jr., "The Ethical Demands for Integration," *A Testament of Hope: The Essential Writings of Martin Luther King, Jr.,* ed. James M. Washington (San Francisco: Harper SanFrancisco, 1986), 120.

[7]King, "The Three Dimensions of a Complete Life," *Knock*, 130.

[8]King, "Facing the Challenge of a New Age," *Testament*, 141.

face attitudes of arrogance and pride, and bitterness and hatred, in the people around us. We will even face systems that institutionalize these attitudes and do all they can to destroy the beloved community we hope to build.[9] For King, these obstructions are not for us to ignore or dismiss—they are for us to overcome.

There Comes a Time

King strongly believed that when we face the obstructions of oppression, we should not roll over and let them kill our creative efforts. Rather, we must hold our heads high, our shoulders back, and protest as loudly and effectively as we can, trusting all the while that we have a moral obligation to resist evil.[10]

We must, therefore, come to realize that there is a breaking point in life when we just cannot and should not take oppression any longer. That was the situation that Rosa Parks faced in her own refusal to abide by the laws of segregation on Montgomery's buses. "One can never understand the action of Mrs. Parks," King stated, "until one realizes that eventually the cup of endurance runs over, and the human personality cries out, 'I can't take it no longer.'"[11]

King led the battle cry. In the very first meeting of the Montgomery Improvement Association (MIA), called in response to the arrest of Parks, he stood before a throng of weary and worn people and cried out in their behalf.

> And you know, my friends, there comes a time when people get tired of being trampled over by the iron feet of oppression. *[Sustained applause]* There comes a time, my friends, when people get tired of being plunged across the abyss of humiliation, where they experience the bleakness

---

[9]Like Reinhold Niebuhr, King found the individual to be much more capable of moral action than social groups. But, unlike Niebuhr, he never really stated the reasons underlying the difference between, as Niebuhr put it, "moral man and immoral society." For more on King's understanding of Niebuhr, see King, "Reinhold Niebuhr's Ethical Dualism," *Papers*, 2: 141–51.

[10]It is possible to trace this lesson to, among others, Daddy King, who protested segregation throughout King's young life, and Benjamin Mays, the president of Morehouse College during King's years there. For more on the roots of King's notion of resistance, see John Ansbro, *Martin Luther King, Jr.: Nonviolent Strategies and Tactics for Social Change* (Lanham, Md.: Madison Books, 2000; reprint 1982), 110–62.

[11]King, *Autobiography*, 50.

of nagging despair. *(Keep talking)* There comes a time when people get tired of being pushed out of the glittering sunlight of life's July and left standing amid the piercing chill of an alpine November. *(That's right) [Applause]* There comes a time.[12]

For King, if we just sit around and wait for life to get better on its own, the iron feet of oppression will trample over us, bleakness will overtake us, and we will freeze to death in the alpine chill. But we are too good to die that way—each of us is *somebody*. The image of God is within us, we are each a being of invaluable spirit, and we are "born for the stars and created for eternity." Just so, our challenge is to see and accept ourselves as downright precious in the sight of God. No matter what others say, no matter what social systems would have us believe, we must see ourselves as individuals God loves and treasures.

So when the breaking point comes, the best we can do is to let it come. Rather than holding it back any longer, we must let the cup of endurance run over and then stand up and cry out. For King, this is what time is for—protesting assaults on our character, our loved ones, and our efforts to build and be part of the beloved community. Time is for crying *No!*

Silence Is Betrayal

King believed that when the time comes, we must shout *No!* from the depths of our soul. King deeply appreciated Black Power for this very reason—it encouraged, and empowered, blacks to cry out, as they never had before, about the injustices they suffered, the oppression that kept them second-class citizens, the degradation they felt from whites. As King saw it, Black Power was the cry of disappointment resulting from hundreds of years of being a pent-up, and silenced, people.[13]

Indeed, he preferred the bellicosity of Black Power activists to the silence of so-called good white people. King had no time for

---

[12]Martin Luther King Jr., "Address to the First Montgomery Improvement Association (MIA) Mass Meeting," *A Call to Conscience: The Landmark Speeches of Dr. Martin Luther King, Jr.,* ed. Clayborne Carson and Kris Shepard (New York: Warner Books, 2001), 9.

[13]For more on his reaction to Black Power, see Martin Luther King Jr., *Where Do We Go from Here: Chaos or Community?* (Boston: Beacon Press, 1968), 23–66.

pious believers who refused to cry out, citing selflessness or righteousness along the way. In his view, crying out is not a selfish act, but rather an act that frees the spirit from bondage so that we can begin to live a creative life that would benefit all. Further, crying out does not mean that we are shouting down people, things, and events just for the sake of shouting them down. When we cry out in faithful protest, according to King, we cry out for the best of reasons—the dignity of the individual and the sacredness of the beloved community.

Thus, silence in the face of oppression, either our own or others', is as bad as the original cause of oppression. When we are silent, we are not faithful to our own dignity or to the God who created us with dignity. "A time comes," King proclaimed, "when silence is betrayal."[14] When he spoke these prophetic words, King was reflecting on his own silence in light of the evils of the Vietnam War—a silence that, as he came to understand it, was a betrayal of the nonviolent love of God he saw in Jesus, the poor peasants being killed by U.S. forces, and his own faith. With this betrayal in mind, King knew that the time had come, as it does in all lives, to cry out against the injustice of humanity.

Time to Stand Up

Moreover, it is not sufficient for us to protest into a vacuum of existence. We must also locate the sources that keep pouring hot water into the cup, even while it runs onto our lap. And when we find them, we must rebuke them directly, accepting along the way that sometimes our cries will have no direct results, or worse, results that are more evil than our present conditions. As a realist, King knew that human history is full of examples of powerful people who ignored the cries of the oppressed, or used them as reasons to ratchet up the oppression. He feared, too, what the powerful know all too well—dead people do not cry.

This is why King believed that when we face oppressors who ignore our cries, or use them as reasons to inflict additional suffering, the time has come for us to stand up and use our bodies to protest.

---

[14]Martin Luther King Jr., "Beyond Vietnam," *A Call to Conscience*, 140. King was quoting the opening words of a statement of the Executive Committee of Clergy and Laymen Concerned about Vietnam.

In King's thought, a life of creative action is not only spiritual; it is also physical, relentlessly physical.

Are We Fit to Live?

It is well-known that King did not favor the use of physical violence against oppressors. For him, the life and death of Jesus taught, and showed, that nonviolence is the way, the truth, and the life. King believed that when Jesus faced his own oppressors, he suffered unflinchingly, even to the point of death, and that Jesus' followers, indeed the world, should do no less than adopt nonviolence as a lifestyle, recognizing not only the practical point that violence begets merely violence, but also the spiritual argument that violence is a sin against the love of God revealed in the crucified Jesus.[15]

King thus insisted that, even as we physically protest the most recalcitrant and intransigent of sinners, we must always remain nonviolent. This does not mean that we must run away from the source of our oppression, though that may be a temporary solution to safeguard our lives; nor does it mean passive acceptance of evil. Far from a "do-nothing method," nonviolent resistance is active— aggressively active: "For while the non-violent resister is passive in the sense that he is not physically aggressive toward his opponent," King argued, "his mind and emotions are always active, constantly seeking to persuade his opponent that he is wrong."[16]

Though he did not say so in this passage, King obviously believed that the body is also constantly active in the nonviolent approach. Remember the men and women, and boys and girls, marching on the dusty roads on the hottest summer days in their quest to resist those who undermined the beloved community. Recall police officers twisting King's arm every which way as they pushed and pulled him

---

[15]For more on King and nonviolence, see Ansbro, *Martin Luther King, Jr.*; James P. Hanigan, *Martin Luther King, Jr., and the Foundations of Nonviolence* (Lanham, Md.: University Press of America, 1984); Greg Moses, *Revolution of Conscience: Martin Luther King, Jr., and the Philosophy of Nonviolence* (New York: The Guilford Press, 1997); and William Watley, *Roots of Resistance: The Nonviolent Ethic of Martin Luther King, Jr.* (Valley Forge, Pa.: Judson Press, 1985). For a contextual contrast to King's nonviolence, see James Cone, *Martin & Malcolm & America* (Maryknoll, N.Y.: Orbis Books, 1991).

[16]King, "An Experiment in Love," *Testament*, 18.

toward their cars and jails. Remember him lying on the ground just after he was shot in Memphis.

For King, there does come a time when we must place our whole bodies—our very lives—into the protest against oppression, and this raises the question of questions: Is there something that we are willing to die for? Have we found something that we would sacrifice our lives for as we face those who refuse to heed our cries? King hoped so: "I say to you…that if you have never found something so dear and so precious that you will die for it, then you aren't fit to live." If we refuse to place our bodies on the line because of fear, or because we want to live a long life, we are already dead. "And the cessation of breathing in your life is but the belated announcement of an earlier death of the spirit. You died when you refused to stand up for right. You died when you refused to stand up for truth. You died when you refused to stand up for justice."[17]

Love Builds Up, and Hate Tears Down

King's advice was clear: Stand up and fight. King himself stood up and fought in a variety of ways. Sometimes he marched against his oppressors, other times he stood up to them in backroom meetings while his followers boycotted them on the streets, and still other times he grabbed a bullhorn on their front steps and demanded that they let his people go.[18] But, whatever specific methods he used, he always insisted on using nonviolent love as his primary weapon. No, he insisted, we do not have to *like* the people, things, or events that seek to prevent us from doing the will of God. But, like Jesus, we do have to *love* our enemies along the way.

> Now we can see what Jesus meant when he said, "Love your enemies." We should be happy that he did not say, "Like your enemies." It is almost impossible to like some people. "Like" is a sentimental and affectionate word. How can we be affectionate toward a person whose avowed aim is to crush our very being and place innumerable stumbling blocks in our path? How can we like a person who is

---

[17]King, *Autobiography*, 344.
[18]For more on the methods of King's nonresistance, see Ansbro, *Martin Luther King, Jr.*, 110–62.

threatening our children and bombing our homes? That is impossible. But Jesus recognized that *love* is greater than *like*. When Jesus bids us to love our enemies, he is speaking neither of *eros* nor *philia*; he is speaking of *agape*, understanding and creative, redemptive goodwill for all men. Only by following this way and responding with this type of love are we able to be children of our Father who is in heaven.[19]

So let us love our enemies, making sure that we never inflict injury on them, physically or spiritually, and that we defeat only their destructive purposes and their systems of support. Let us make sure, too, that we always see the image of God within them, that we separate the sinner from the sin, that we see them as our brothers and sisters, and that we seek their reconciliation within the community of divine love. Always, that is, let us embody *agape*.[20] "*Agape* is love seeking to preserve and create community... *Agape* is a willingness to go to any length to restore community."[21]

Only by practicing *agape* can we be true to our identity and to the identity of the human race. On the one hand, King believed that

---

[19]King, "Loving Your Enemies," *Strength*, 50.

[20]Note that there is no qualification on this point; King firmly believed that we should always seek reconciliation. In reply to an *Ebony* reader who had offended her minister, King stated: "Remember, a true Christian is willing to go to any length to restore brotherly relationships," in King, "Advice for Living," *Symbol of the Movement, January 1957–December 1958*, vol. 4 of *The Papers of Martin Luther King, Jr.*, ed. Clayborne Carson et al. (Berkeley: University of California Press, 2000), 521.

[21]King, "An Experiment in Love," *Testament*, 30. For more on his understanding of nonviolence and its relationship to love, see King, "Love, Law, and Civil Disobedience," *Testament*, 43–53; and "An Experiment in Love," *Testament*, 16–20. The latter resource details King's six "basic facts" about the method of nonviolent resistance. First, nonviolent resistance resists evil. Second, it seeks not to defeat opponents but to establish reconciliation with them. Third, nonviolent resistance attacks the forces of evil, not the individuals who actually do the evil. Fourth, it accepts suffering, emotional and physical, without "striking back." Fifth, nonviolent resistance avoids both "external physical violence" and "internal violence of the spirit." Sixth, it is carried out with "the conviction that the universe is on the side of justice," and that God will make all things whole. As a form of Christian love, nonviolent resistance, as King understood it, is sacrificial, forgiving, reconciling, and peaceful. For more on the sources of King's understanding of love, see Keith Miller, *Voice of Deliverance: The Language of Martin Luther King Jr. and Its Sources* (New York: The Free Press, 1992), 59–60.

we should love our enemies as Jesus loved his because that is what God has created us to do: God has created us in the divine image so that we can live nobly, creatively, and nonviolently in relation to others. On the other hand, as noted earlier, King believed that we should love our enemies because they, like all of us, have the image of God within them. Even as a graduate student, King had maintained that the worst of humanity enjoys the image of God. Criticizing the theologies of John Calvin and Martin Luther on this point, King wrote: "Certainly we must agree that the image of God is terribly scarred in man, but not to the degree that man cannot move toward God." More fundamentally, King believed that Jesus "constantly made appeal to a hidden goodness in their nature."[22] Yes, humanity is deeply sinful, in King's thought, but never wholly depraved, exactly because God places the divine image within each and every person.

King insisted on the presence of *agape* also because he recognized that standing up against oppression, in and of itself, is not necessarily a creative act. In fact, resisting for the sake of resisting, or for the sake of vengeance, is not a moral act at all; what makes resistance moral, and ultimately focused on creativity, is the presence of *agape* in our methods and goals. Ultimately, creative *agape* is also the most practical and durable resource we could ever adopt in our efforts to build the beloved community. In response to an *Ebony* reader who encouraged him to concede that love is "impractical," and that sometimes it is best to "fight fire with fire," King replied:

> I am convinced that love is the most durable power in the world. It is not an expression of impractical idealism; but of practical realism. Far from being the pious injunction of a Utopian dreamer, love is an absolute necessity for the survival of our civilization. To return hate for hate does nothing but intensify the existence of evil in the universe. Someone must have sense enough and religion enough to cut off the chain of hate and evil, and this can only be done through love. Moreover, love is creative and redemptive. Love builds up and unites; hate tears down and destroys. That aftermath of

---

[22]King, "A Comparison and Evaluation of the Theology of Luther with That of Calvin," *Papers*, 2: 190.

the "fight fire with fire" method which you suggest is bitterness and chaos; the aftermath of the love method is reconciliation and the creation of the beloved community. Physical force can repress, restrain, coerce, destroy, but it cannot create and organize anything permanent; only love can do that. Yes, love—which means understanding, creative, redemptive goodwill, even for one's enemies—is the solution to the race problem. Often love is crucified and buried in a grave, but in the long run it rises up and redeems even that which crucifies it.[23]

A Little Help from Our Friends

Moreover, King also insisted that when we stand up in love, we should always rely on others to help us overcome the obstructions. Standing up is not the work of a virtuoso. We need our brothers and sisters at all times, especially when we face violent oppressors whose violent ways, after all, can easily snuff out one person.

Further, sometimes we need to turn to allies more powerful than the sisters and brothers right next to us. Sometimes the violence is so bad, for example, that we need the power of government to protect us. King did not want us to grab our violent enemies with our own hands, but he did concede that if we are going to march full force toward the beloved community, we will sometimes need the police to stand with us and pry murderous hands off our necks.[24] King himself often turned to the state and federal governments for protection from violent oppressors, including members of local police

[23]Martin Luther King Jr., "Advice for Living," *Papers,* 4:305–6.

[24]For more on King's relationship to the powers of the state, see Lewis V. Baldwin, "On the Relation of the Church to the State: The Development of a Kingian Ethic," in Lewis V. Baldwin with Rufus Burrow Jr., Barbara A. Holmes, and Susan Holmes Winfield, *The Legacy of Martin Luther King, Jr.: The Boundaries of Law, Politics, and Religion* (Notre Dame, Ind.: University of Notre Dame Press, 2002), 77–123; Michael Eric Dyson, *I May Not Get There With You: The True Martin Luther King, Jr.* (New York: The Free Press, 2000); Michael G. Long, *Against Us, But for Us: Martin Luther King, Jr., and the State* (Macon, Ga.: Mercer University Press, 2002) ; and John T. McCartney, *Black Power Ideologies: An Essay in African-American Political Thought* (Philadelphia: Temple University Press, 1992).

forces throughout the South. More particularly, he frequently called upon the National Guard and U.S. federal marshals to protect him and his followers from the death threats they continually faced on their march toward the beloved community.[25]

Beyond that, King recognized that systemic problems require systemic solutions. This means that when we stand up and protest problems like discrimination and segregation, one of the best things we can do is to demand that our government assume an active role in addressing the problems.[26] Sometimes only social systems, like the government, possess the *power* and resources required for successfully eliminating the systemic obstructions we face. In other words, no matter what we may believe about our own abilities, sometimes we just do not have everything it takes to carry out successful resistance.

To do the will of God, then, is to cry out against injustice, to stand up and use our bodies to back our cries, and to rely on others who have the power required for eliminating the obstructions we face in creating the beloved community. But King was careful to note that we should beware that there is grave danger in crying out and standing up. Sacrifice, suffering, and possibly death await those who protest against powerful people and institutions. But, for King, that does not matter. What ultimately matters is that we do the will of God, come what may—that we act for God in the moment.

King, however, was too positive a thinker to stop at this point; for in his view, crying out and using our bodies to overturn obstructions are inherently negative actions, far from the ultimate

---

[25]King thought it legitimate for the state to use forcible means to ensure protection of citizens seeking the beloved community. In his view, the state's use of force was an issue of justice: The state that forcibly fights unjust disorder mirrors the God of justice. For more on this, see Long, *Against Us, But for Us*, 107–12. Interestingly, King never used the word *love* when explaining his belief that the state should sometimes use forcible means to establish a social order with peace and justice.

[26]Underlying his qualified embrace of government is the following political conviction: "Man is not made for the state; the state is made for man," Martin Luther King Jr., *Stride Toward Freedom: The Montgomery Story* (New York: Harper & Row, 1958), 93. This quotation directly reflects the work of the French political philosopher Jacques Maritain.

goal of our lives. In other words, they are just the first steps on our march toward the beloved community.[27]

Character and Community

For King, the march may begin with negative acts—crying out and standing up—but it quickly moves to the positive act of creation. King's creative emphasis is especially visible in his understanding of the three positive ingredients of the beloved community— integration, peace, and economic justice.

King emphasized time and again that there is a significant difference between desegregation and integration. As he saw it, desegregation is "eliminative and negative"; it simply removes the legal and social prohibitions embedded in the prohibitive system of segregation. Destructive in nature, desegregation is only a means to a constructive end—integration. "Integration is genuine intergroup, interpersonal doing." It is the positive act through which people welcome one another as equal members in the human family.[28]

King held a somewhat similar view in his understanding of the difference between negative peace and true peace. Negative peace is "the absence of tension." It is important because it provides people with the opportunity to coexist without killing one another, but negative peace is exactly that—negative. The ultimate goal—true peace—is creative and constructive: "True peace is not merely the absence of tension, but it is the presence of justice and brotherhood." Negative peace makes for a "stagnant passivity and deadening complacency," but true peace can establish the reign of God, the beloved community.[29]

King felt the same way about the third ingredient of the beloved community—economic justice. Economic justice is much more than

---

[27]For more on King's understanding of the steps of resistance, see John C. Raines, "Righteous Resistance and Martin Luther King Jr.," *Christian Century* 101 (January 18, 1984): 52–54. It is important to note, however, that Raines overstates his case when he states that the first step of resistance is "to see things as they really are, to stop dreaming and to stand together" (53). For King, dreaming is the substance of the end of the resistance, and, just so, it preexists in the means of resistance.

[28]King, "The Ethical Demands for Integration," *Testament*, 118.

[29]King, "Love, Law, and Civil Disobedience," *Testament*, 51.

the destruction of slums; it is also the construction of affordable, high-quality housing for residents who have power (voice and vote) in decision-making about the rules and regulations of their neighborhoods. In addition, economic justice is more than the elimination of dead-end jobs; it is also the creation of jobs and careers with livable wages for workers who have power in decision-making about the rules and regulations governing their work.

For King, then, it is not enough for us to destroy obstructions to the beloved community: As co-*creators* with God, we must begin to *create* positive attitudes and institutions that will make the beloved community a reality. Yes, the elimination of the obstructions is necessary, but because we are born for the stars and created for eternity, the nature of our work must ultimately be noble, good, and creative.

This also means that it is not good enough just to dream. Dreams without works are dead, empty, shallow, nothing more than abstract fantasies, and so dreams are for living out, making real. The path of creative living thus moves from the removal of oppression, through our dreams, and into the positive creation of the beloved community.[30] More particularly, creative living seeks to make our dreams come alive in the reality of our everyday life—in both personal character and social justice—so that we can better recognize and serve the will of God. As King put this, "Our hope for creative living lies in our ability to reestablish the spiritual ends of our lives in personal character and social justice."[31]

Time to Develop Moral Character

When we dream, we must imagine not only a new world out there in the community around us, but also a new world inside of us. In King's view, the beloved community is grounded in personal

---

[30]Kenneth Smith's words are instructive here: "It would be a mistake to remember King as *just* a dreamer—someone who only *contemplated* his dreams. His dreams were always related to strategies and actions," in "Incorporating the Dream of Martin Luther King, Jr.," *Christian Century* 105 (April 6, 1988): 333. James A. Colaiaco offers a similar point: "But King was not a mere dreamer, setting ideals for humanity; he was also a doer, a drum major for freedom, justice and equality, leading and inspiring many to take practical steps toward the attainment of these ideals," in *Martin Luther King, Jr.: Apostle of Militant Nonviolence* (New York: St. Martin's Press, 1988), 203.

[31]King, "The Man Who Was a Fool," *Strength*, 74–75.

character. Indeed, if the community is ever to flourish, we must first develop a character that reflects our God-given dignity and the love and justice of God.

It is thus simply not enough for us to know about the beloved community; our whole character must embody the guiding virtues and goals of the community. Even as a student at Morehouse in 1947, King addressed the issue of education and character: "We must remember," he wrote in the college newspaper, "that intelligence is not enough. Intelligence plus character—that is the goal of true education."[32]

When speaking of moral character in later years, King often noted his special concern that segregation had created personal and cultural problems within the lives of his black sisters and brothers, and so their unique challenge, as he understood it, was not only to replace the system of segregation but also to address the internal problems caused by the system. "Let us be honest with ourselves," King stated, "and say that…our standards have lagged behind at many points."[33] The problems were real—high crime rates, black-on-black murder, and welfare dependency. King could have pointed his finger merely elsewhere, but, in addition to calling for help from the government, he also counseled moral character work within the black community itself: "We've got to lift our moral standards at every hand, at every point…the great thing about life is that any man can be good, and honest, and ethical, and moral, and can have character."[34]

Indeed, he called upon all people to "have character." King was certainly not the type of character ethicist we know today in such figures as Stanley Hauerwas and his students.[35] Unlike them, King had no developed theology of character, but he did have a general understanding of the type of character that would be faithful to

[32]Martin Luther King Jr., "The Purpose of Education," *Called to Serve: January 1929–June 1951,* vol. 1 of *The Papers of Martin Luther King, Jr.*, ed. Clayborne Carson et al. (Berkeley: University of California Press, 1992), 124.

[33]Martin Luther King Jr., "Some Things We Must Do," *Papers,* 4: 335.

[34]Ibid., 336.

[35]A good starting point for exploring Hauerwas's work is his *Community of Character* (Notre Dame, Ind.: University of Notre Dame Press, 1981).

both God and the civil rights movement—a character sketched in the "ten commandments" that he asked civil rights volunteers in Birmingham to follow:

1. Meditate daily on the teachings and life of Jesus.
2. Remember always that the nonviolent movement in Birmingham seeks justice and reconciliation—not victory.
3. Walk and talk in the manner of love, for God is love.
4. Pray daily to be used by God in order that all men might be free.
5. Sacrifice personal wishes in order that all men might be free.
6. Observe with both friend and foe the ordinary rules of courtesy.
7. Seek to perform regular service for others and for the world.
8. Refrain from the violence of fist, tongue, or heart.
9. Seek to be in good spiritual and bodily health.
10. Follow the directions of the movement and of the captain on a demonstration.[36]

For King, then, to "have character" is to reflect the life of Jesus by embracing, and practicing, the virtues of faith, hope, love, sacrifice, peace, and justice. Only when we have this type of character are we then prepared to serve the will of God through the civil rights movement.

Further, only when we embrace these virtues can the beloved community even begin to flourish as God intends.[37] For example, integration will never flourish until we embrace the virtue of love deep in our hearts so that we can truly welcome one another as brothers and sisters in the one human family. Economic justice will never flourish until we allow the virtue of justice to reign in our hearts so that we can courageously fight the evil of poverty, as well as the evil of an unjust legal system. Peace, too, will never flourish

[36]Martin Luther King Jr., *Why We Can't Wait* (New York: New American Library, 1963), 63–64.

[37]I agree with Anthony E. Cook, *The Least of These: Race, Law, and Religion in American Culture* (New York: Routledge, 1997), 111–12: "King understood that the new laws put in place by the civil rights movement were, in and of themselves, no guarantee of a just and loving community. Rather, the individuals promulgating, enforcing, interpreting, and following those laws must themselves be just and loving individuals. King understood, as Dewey came ultimately to see, that democratic institutions were no substitute for democratic individuals."

until we become wholly peaceful in the deepest recesses of our hearts—peaceful with ourselves and others.

For King, this is especially where the work of schools and faith communities enters. A key, and unique, role of education and religion, in King's view, is to transform the affections of people's hearts. [38] Yes, government can change external behavior through the incentives and disincentives of legislation, but it is extremely limited in changing internal attitudes. Schools and faith communities, however, are not so limited. Indeed, one of their primary roles is to develop moral character that reflects the virtues of the beloved community. As King put this in his *Ebony* column, "We need laws to change the habits of men while we wait on religion and education to change their hearts." [39] And until schools and faith communities assume their proper role in character formation, integration, let alone peace and economic justice, will remain elusive, and schools and faith communities themselves will lack character. [40]

It is simply not possible to underestimate the role of faith communities in King's understanding of character formation, primarily because, as the above "ten commandments" suggest, King envisioned an inextricable relationship between "having character" and "following the will God." To have character, in his view, is first and foremost a matter of believing in God and surrendering ourselves—our passions and interests—to the divine will. King explained this point when an *Ebony* reader asked him for advice for overcoming a bad temper. Using the traditional language of moral character theory, with its references to virtues and vices, King replied:

> You expel a lower vice by concentrating on a higher virtue. If you will continually concentrate on the necessity of being calm and even tempered you will soon remove your nasty temper by this higher concentration. A destructive passion is harnessed by directing the same passion into constructive channels. Finally, you should submit your will to the power and scrutiny of God. *Ultimately one is changed by surrendering*

---

[38]On the role of the heart in character ethics, see Richard Bondi, "The Elements of Character," *Journal of Religious Ethics* 12, no. 4 (1984): 201–18.

[39]King, "Advice for Living," *Papers*, 4: 542.

[40]See King, *Stride*, 205.

his will to God's will. You cannot solve the problem alone. You must realize the need for depending on a higher power.[41]

King appeals here to the psychological practice of channeling as a method of character formation, but his primary point is that moral character ultimately has spiritual roots: Only by believing in, depending on, and acting faithfully in response to God can we mold our characters in a way that serves not only our own lives but also the life of the beloved community. Without God, in King's thought, our characters will remain maladjusted, and our community will remain broken.

King attributed the depth of his own character to his trust in the abiding presence of God in his life. When an *Ebony* reader asked him for advice on ways that others could achieve the inner peace and calm that he exuded after he was stabbed in New York, King took the occasion to describe the connection he saw between his moral character, with its virtue of courage, and his dependence on God:

> If I demonstrated unusual calm during the recent attempt on my life, it was certainly not due to any extraordinary powers that I possess. Rather, it was due to the power of God working through me. Throughout this struggle for racial justice I have constantly asked God to remove all bitterness from my heart and to give me strength and courage to face any disaster that came my way. This constant prayer life and feeling of dependence on God have given me the feeling that I have divine companionship in the struggle. I know of no other way to explain it. It is the fact that in the midst of external tension, God can give an inner peace.[42]

King's reply here clearly suggests not only the general point that believing in God is key to character development, but also the more specific point that the practice of prayer is an indispensable way to build character. We can help develop the character God desires for us, in King's thought, by entering into a prayer life in which we

---

[41]King, "Advice for Living," *Papers*, 4: 269 (emphasis mine).
[42]King, "Advice for Living," *Papers*, 4: 540.

surrender our wills to God, imploring God to help us eliminate our vices and take on the divine virtues of love, justice, and peace. We simply cannot form character alone—we desperately need God, the source of love and justice; and God is available to us through prayer. For King, then, the discipline of prayer is not only helpful but also necessary for becoming the whole person each of us can be.

Yet another key dimension of King's understanding of moral character formation is the practice of apprenticeship. The tenth commandment mentioned above calls upon the would-be civil rights worker to "follow the directions of the movement and of the captain on a demonstration." This commandment may seem a bit out of place, especially in relation to the previous nine, some of which are explicitly spiritual, like the one on prayer, but character ethicists have long recognized that the concrete practice of apprenticeship— placing ourselves under the authority of a skilled and virtuous leader—is necessary for our moral development.[43] Having seen his own character molded by his beloved family members and teachers, King believed the same: If we want to strengthen our moral character, in his view, we should apprentice ourselves to a good person. More particularly, if we want to have a good Christian character, we should apprentice ourselves to a faithful Christian—a man or woman who speaks the moral language of Christianity fluently, who uses the tools of Christianity with expertise, and who lives out the practices of Christianity better than anyone we know. More specifically, as apprentices, we would do well to observe and imitate the moral leaders, saying what they say and doing what they do.

Creative living, then, is all about apprenticing ourselves to mentors who can lead us into belief and deepen our faith in God so that we can have the character required for the flourishing of the beloved community—character marked by the virtues of peace, love, and justice. In addition, creative living means inviting people to become *our* apprentices so that we can build the beloved community by strengthening the moral character of individuals who seek to grow in, and give expression to, their faith. Clearly, King sought to do both. On the one hand, he apprenticed himself to people like

---

[43]For a contemporary expression of this point, see Stanley Hauerwas, *After Christendom?—How the Church Is to Behave if Freedom, Justice, and a Christian Nation Are Bad Ideas* (Nashville: Abingdon Press, 1991), 101–7.

Daddy King and Benjamin Mays, gigantic spiritual mentors who could show him the Way. On the other hand, he encouraged people like Andrew Young and Jesse Jackson to become his own apprentices so that they, too, might carry on the work of the beloved community that King had begun. King sought to do both simply because of his fundamental belief that the beloved community rests on and emerges from the moral character of the individuals who would dare to build and reside in the community that God intends.

Confident Living

Though he highlighted the need to develop personal character, King did not want us to become lost in ourselves. Self-obsession is not a virtue at all in King's thought. On the contrary, his vision of doing the will of God, come what may, is primarily a matter of lifting up the dignity of our sisters and brothers. Indeed, having character, in King's thought, means not only loving ourselves, but especially desiring to serve the neighbors we love.

King expressed his cautionary note on self-obsession in response to a young male *Ebony* reader with a crisis in self-confidence. King's reply to the socially challenged young man set forth four practices as a guide to "confident living": Know your potentialities and limitations, accept yourself as a unique somebody, trust in your abilities, and deny yourself. For King, the last point was key. "You probably lose confidence in yourself," he stated, "because you are thinking too much about yourself." Proposing a remedy, King suggested that the young man think of ways to make others happy, especially those he was close to. "Soon," King suggested, "you will find that you spend so much time thinking of others that you have little time to think of yourself. There is so much more to think about than ourselves."[44]

Make a Career of Humanity

King thus believed that when we do the will of God, come what may, we ultimately lose ourselves in creative service to others, even as we seek to build our own moral character. When advising young people at a 1959 youth march for integrated schools, King

---

[44]King, "Advice for Living," *Papers,* 4: 472.

suggested exactly this—that they devote themselves to serving their neighbor. "Make a career of humanity," he said. To do the will of God is to build up the human potential in everyone we face. The benefits of serving humanity are not only for those we serve, though; they are also for us: "It will give you that rare sense of nobility that can only spring from love and selflessly helping your fellow man."[45]

By imploring the young people to make a career of *humanity*, King was clearly steering them away from a life focused on acquiring and consuming *things*. As a young man, King clearly liked the sharp cars and clothes that his family could afford, but Coretta Scott King notes that, as he immersed himself ever more deeply into the fight for civil rights, he began to let go of the things that he had enjoyed in earlier years. Her memory on this important point for creative living is worth quoting in full:

> He grew in his certainty that he did not want to own things, that money and material success meant less and less to him. As the years went by, Martin really wished to take a vow of poverty. He was forced by his position as a family man to temper this desire, but even so, he did not want those possessions which would separate him from the masses. He would say such things as, 'I don't see why we have to own a house.' When he began his ministry, he had felt that clothes were important in representing his congregation. As the years went by, he discarded that view completely and boasted that he could travel around the world without a suitcase, with one suit only and a change of underwear. Martin always tried to eliminate from our own lives all things we could do without, and he hoped to influence his followers to do the same.[46]

Living creatively thus means, on the one hand, eliminating unnecessary things from our life, and on the other hand, serving our neighbor—a practice that, according to King, we have no reason to refuse.

---

[45]King, *Autobiography*, 138.
[46]Coretta Scott King, *My Life with Martin Luther King, Jr.* (New York: Holt Rinehart & Winston, 1969), 160–61.

You don't have to have a college degree to serve. You don't have to make your subject and verb agree to serve. You don't have to know about Plato and Aristotle to serve. You don't have to know Einstein's theory of relativity to serve. You don't have to know the second theory of thermodynamics in physics to serve. You only need a heart full of grace. A soul generated by love. And you can be that servant.[47]

So where to start our service to humanity? For King, the answer is clear—right where we are. King did not believe that it is always necessary for us to leave behind our jobs or careers in order to serve humanity, or even to make a career of humanity. On the contrary, he stressed that part of our life mission is to strive for excellence in our chosen fields of labor. Speaking at Holt Street Baptist Church in 1957, King stated that no matter what our jobs are, we must do them as well as we can.[48]

Do it so well that the living, the dead, or the unborn *(Yes)* can't do it better. *(Yeah)* If it falls to your lot to be a street sweeper, sweep streets like Raphael painted pictures; sweep streets like Michelangelo carved marble; sweep streets like Beethoven composed music; sweep streets like Shakespeare wrote poetry; sweep streets so well that all the hosts of heaven and earth will have to pause and say: "Here lived a great street sweeper *(All right)*, who swept his job well." *(Oh yes).*[49]

---

[47]King, "The Drum Major Instinct," *Testament*, 265–66.

[48]King strongly believed in working for a living and criticized practices that undermined the value of labor. In reply to an *Ebony* reader who asked about the morality of gambling, King stated: "One should live by the principle that he will not take from society without giving to it," King, "Advice for Living," *Papers*, 4: 280. Gambling, he believed, undermines this principle: It takes without giving. King stressed the value of all labor in "The Three Dimensions of a Complete Life," *Knock*, 125: After preaching that people should discover what they are called to do, King stated: "Now, this does not mean that everybody will do the so-called big, recognized things of life. Very few people will rise to the heights of genius in the arts and the sciences, very few collectively will rise to certain professions. Most of us will have to be content to work in the fields and in the factories and on the streets. But we must see the dignity of all labor. *(That's right)*."

[49]King, "Some Things We Must Do," *Papers*, 4: 338.

But for King, excellence also means doing our jobs in a way that *always* serves humanity. Robbing dignity from our neighbors at work and then seeking to establish justice for them in charitable works on the weekend or in retirement is simply destructive, both to ourselves and to our neighbors. Truly creative living means serving humanity at all times and in all places, including the workplace. As King put it to the students at the march for integrated schools, "Whatever career you may choose for yourself—doctor, lawyer, teacher—let me propose an avocation to be pursued *along with it*. Become a dedicated fighter for civil rights. Make it a central part of your life."[50]

If we are street cleaners, then, let us love all the neighbors whose dirt we sweep away, and seek justice for them by making the world a clean place for living. Or if we are doctors, let us treat all of our patients with love, and seek justice for them by making the world a healthy place. We participate in creative living when we use our unique gifts—our particular intelligence, courage, and bodily strength—to serve humanity in loving and just ways wherever we are.

Time to Create Social Institutions

But King did emphasize that, if we are to make a career of humanity, it is necessary for us to be intentional about creating social institutions—families, schools, churches, voluntary agencies, and governments—where the beloved community can take root and begin to grow. This is exactly what the time of our life is for—creating social institutions for the flourishing of the beloved community. At its fullest, then, time is for molding our personal character in accord with the love and justice of God so that we can create structures of the beloved community wherever we find ourselves.

Social institutions play a key role in King's thought on creative living. Indeed, King believed that individuals surrounded by unhealthy social institutions had no opportunity at all for creative living; destructive personal lives, in his thought, are often the direct result of social institutions that degrade human dignity. Consider his reply to an *Ebony* reader who asked him for advice on both reducing

---

[50]King, *Autobiography*, 138.

criminality among blacks and discerning the church's role in taking a stand on black crime:

> The Negro is not criminal by nature. Indeed, criminality is environmental, not racial. Poverty and ignorance breed crime whatever the racial group may be. So we must work to remove the system of segregation, discrimination, and the existence of economic injustice if we are to solve the problem of crime in the Negro community. For these external factors are causally responsible for crime. On the other hand, the Negro must work within the community to solve the problem while the external cause factors are being removed. Community agencies and the church must work untiringly to give Negroes moving into the big industrial areas a sense of belonging and help them adjust to urban living.[51]

Social institutions are so important, in King's view, because they directly shape moral character; and this means that morally bankrupt social institutions are so important, and require our attention and action, because they corrupt the moral character of the individuals who move within and through them. Segregated schools, for example, scar the souls and distort the personalities of all the affected children, black and white. Factories that refuse to pay fair wages to, or even hire, black men and women create individuals who turn to a life of crime for their livelihood. And militaristic governments create violent citizens by asking them to hate, and then kill, their enemies.

If we are to live creatively, we must either remove ourselves from those institutions, an option that King did not grant sustained attention to,[52] transform the existing institutions so that they can no longer sustain systems of evil, or create new institutions of love and justice.[53] In other words, if we are to live creatively, we must

---

[51]King, "Advice for Living," *Papers*, 4: 471.

[52]In the last part of his life, King made the case for "temporary segregation" from institutions that practiced integration without giving real power to blacks. See King, *Autobiography*, 325.

[53]King generally favored remaining in existing institutions and seeking to transform them from within. He recommended this practice of internal transformation to Christians who were frustrated with their churches, as well as to American citizens, including Black Power advocates, who were frustrated with U.S. political and economic institutions. In both cases, King called for a revolution from within the existing institutions.

seek to make sure that the social institutions of our community serve humanity. And so this is the question that must always guide us as we seek to live creatively: Do the institutions in our everyday life uplift or degrade the human personality?

Do our families encourage love for those both within and outside the family? Are our schools integrated—truly welcoming of all people? Do our workplaces pay livable wages that allow for their employees to feed, clothe, and give adequate shelter to their family members? Do our medical institutions provide adequate health care for all our community members? Does our government ask us to participate in killing, or in creating social institutions with peace and justice for all?

Just as he believed that social institutions could either create or destroy moral character, King also maintained that social institutions could make or break the community in which we reside. Social institutions, in his thought, have a personal effect on our moral character and a social effect on the character of our community. Thus, the beloved community cannot and will not emerge until we seek to create social institutions marked by love and justice. Without love and justice as their hallmark characteristics, social institutions create only broken communities, not beloved ones.

According to King's social thought, then, integration will not arrive until we build schools where little boys and girls of all backgrounds can study, play, and enjoy snack time together; communities of faith where people of all colors can worship side-by-side, as if they really believe that all people come from one God; and a court system that upholds the rights of all people, especially the rights to life, liberty, and the pursuit of happiness.

Economic justice will not exist until we build schools devoted to helping all students receive the education they need for earning a livable wage; unions that fight for the rights of workers whose employers practice discrimination and pay wages that hover near the poverty line; and governments that guarantee an annual income for those who are unable to work, and that safeguard pensions from employers who would raid them for their own use.

And peace will not come until we create families that seek reconciliation above all material interests; churches where pastors actually preach the cruciform love of Jesus, a nonviolent love that seeks the redemption of everyone; and governments whose foreign policy teams are fully integrated, sensitive to the possibility of race wars, and devoted to practicing nonviolent resistance even in the area of international relations.

In short, the emergence of the beloved community depends upon the presence of social institutions that mirror the love and justice of God.

The Network of Mutuality

If we want to live creatively, then, we must deepen our moral character, ensuring that it is rooted in faith in God, and build social structures that mirror the character of God. As we do so, King would counsel, we must remember that we cannot act alone. What affects one affects all: Each of us is caught in "an inescapable network of mutuality."[54] Further, because the beloved community is so communal, nothing less than communal action is required. With this in mind, King called upon his followers to pull together, form allied partnerships, and seek all the social, political, and economic power required for creating the beloved community. In fact, though he disagreed with its move away from his vision of integration, King deeply appreciated the Black Power movement for its radical commitment to seeking the type of power that would lead to an integrated society where all would enjoy voice and vote in the decisions that would affect one's ability to live creatively in society. By the end of his life, King was emphasizing that creative living requires the creation of *communal power*.

Tomorrow Is Today

The time for creative action is *always*. For King, progress comes only through the "tireless efforts" of individuals who feel passionate about the beloved community. "Without this persistent work," King stated, "time itself becomes an ally of the insurgent and primitive forces of irrational emotionalism and social stagnation."[55] So let us not wait passively, but "help time and realize that the time is always

---

[54]King, "The Man Who Was a Fool," *Strength*, 70. Richard Lischer, *The Preacher King: Martin Luther King, Jr., and the Word That Moved America* (New York: Oxford University Press, 1995), 43, notes that King is indebted for this phrase to Henry Emerson Fosdick.

[55]King, "Love, Law, and Civil Disobedience," *Testament*, 51.

right to do right."[56] Equally important, let us not take long breaks between our creative acts, committing, say, just ten percent of our waking hours to working for the beloved community. Instead, King stated, we should work persistently, indefatigably, for the beloved community. Creative action must be persistent and ongoing—it must move forward without rest.[57] As King liked to say, "This is no time for apathy nor complacency. This is a time for vigorous and positive action."[58]

Moreover, the time for restless creative action is *now*. We should never procrastinate, in King's thought, because when we do so, we surrender to the ongoing rush of time. King realized this especially when reflecting on his own procrastination in response to the Vietnam War. During this difficult period, he counseled others to avoid the same problem:

> We are now faced with the fact, my friends, that tomorrow is today. We are confronted with the fierce urgency of now. In this unfolding conundrum of life and history, there is such a thing as being too late. Procrastination is still the thief of time…We may cry out desperately for time to pause in her passage, but time is adamant to every plea and rushes on. Over the bleached bones and jumbled residues of numerous civilizations are written the pathetic words: "Too late."[59]

Because time rushes on, *now* is the time for creative action. Time will not wait for us to garner all the support we desire, build all the resources we need, or achieve the level of comfort we crave. The nature of time includes the dynamic of movement: It simply rushes on without any regard to our personal preparedness.

Not only does it rush on—time kills. Like Paul Tillich, the subject of his dissertation, King believed that the character of time could be

---

[56]King, "Remaining Awake Through a Great Revolution," *Knock*, 210.
[57]King, "The Social Organization of Nonviolence," *Testament*, 33.
[58]King, "Address Delivered at the National Biennial Convention of the American Jewish Congress," *Papers*, 4: 410.
[59]King, "Beyond Vietnam," *Call*, 162.

annihilating.[60] Without creative action to fill it, time rushes on, pulling life along with it and leaving behind miles of bleached bones; and if all we do is procrastinate, time will do the same to us—it will steal our very life.

This is the reason that King emphasized the urgency of *now*. For King, now is the time when we must choose life or surrender to the forces of death; now is the time when we must act for others or let time pull the very life out of them; and now is the time when time will kill us—unless we *do* something to counter its annihilating character.

Finally, now is the time for *full-force* creative action. King firmly believed that moderation simply would not do.[61] If moderation means acting with appropriate reasonableness and restraint, it is a great virtue, but if it means slowing down our creative action on any level, it is a great vice. That is because when we slow down our creative action, the deadly status quo fills time as it moves on. When the will of God is at stake, then, we just cannot afford to slow down. We must always keep on keeping on: "For the hour is already late," as King stated time and again. "And the clock of destiny is ticking out."[62]

---

[60]See King, "A Comparison of the Conceptions of God in the Thinking of Paul Tillich and Henry Nelson Wieman," (Ph.D. dissertation, Boston University, 1955), *Papers*, 2: 401.

[61]King's most famous statement on moderation is found in his letter from Birmingham Jail. See King, *Autobiography*, 188–204. An excellent account of the substance and context of the letter is S. Jonathan Bass, *Blessed Are the Peacemakers: Martin Luther King, Jr., Eight White Religious Leaders, and the "Letter from Birmingham Jail"* (Baton Rouge: Louisiana State University Press, 2001).

[62]King, "The American Dream," *Knock*, 87.

CHAPTER FOUR

Retreat to the Mountain
Advice for Being

As we keep on keeping on, marching toward the beloved community by building moral character and social institutions that embody the love and justice of God, we may discover that we become so tired that we need to sit down, take a break, and refuel. This is what King discovered, too. His vigorous work on behalf of the beloved community sometimes drove him to the point of sheer exhaustion, and in those moments of feeling utterly worn down, with a tired body and a weary soul, he came to believe that creative living requires not only *doing* but also *being*—taking a break so that we can regain the energy we need for returning to a life of doing.

Going On and On

King was a busy man. "He could go on and on," according to Andrew Young, "when things were going very well."[1] Going on

---

[1] David J. Garrow, *Bearing the Cross: Martin Luther King, Jr., and the Southern Christian Leadership Conference* (New York: Vintage Books, 1986), 602. It is interesting to note here that Coretta Scott King opens her autobiography, *My Life with Martin Luther King, Jr.* (New York: Holt Rinehart & Winston, 1969) by describing the busyness of King's life in 1964; King's busyness is a theme that runs throughout her book.

and on during those periods of success, King would deliver up to thirty speeches a week and survive on only two to four hours of sleep each night. Add on the administrative responsibilities of his position, as well as the toll of the marches, and we can easily understand the reason that his doctors frequently counseled him to slow down, take a break, and go on vacation.

The busyness came as no surprise to King. Indeed, the fear of busyness was partly what initially gave him pause when A.D. Nixon invited him to become an active leader in the looming Montgomery crisis. Facing the arrival of his newborn daughter, Yoki, as well as the overwhelming responsibilities of being a new parish pastor, King feared the severe time constraints that he knew he would face—the same type of constraints that had led him earlier to decline the presidency of the local NAACP.

But King could not resist the Spirit of Montgomery, and shortly after he accepted the presidency of the Montgomery Improvement Association, he experienced exactly what he had predicted—an overwhelming sense of busyness. By his own account, demands on his time tripled upon assuming leadership of the movement, and that was just the beginning, as indicated in his farewell message to Dexter Avenue Baptist Church:

> As a result of my leadership in the Montgomery movement, my duties and activities tripled. A multiplicity of new responsibilities poured in upon me in almost staggering torrents. So I ended up futilely attempting to be four or five men in one. One would have expected that many of these responsibilities would have tapered off after the boycott. But now, three years after the termination of the bus struggle, the same situation stands.[2]

King bid farewell to Dexter in 1959 because he believed that by becoming co-pastor at Ebenezer Baptist Church in Atlanta, where Daddy King acted as the senior pastor and main administrative leader, he would be able to counter the problem of busyness in his life. "I thought," King said, "that I would have more time to meditate and

---

[2]Martin Luther King Jr., *The Autobiography of Martin Luther King, Jr.*, ed. Clayborne Carson (New York: Warner Books, 1998), 136.

think through the total struggle ahead. Unfortunately, however, things happened which made my schedule more crowded in Atlanta than it was in Montgomery."[3] In fact, from the early movement days to the last of his life, the time demands seemed to increase all the more. The more well-known King became, the more others wanted him in their lives, and the more he was present in their lives, sacrificing his own time and life for the good of theirs, the more he wanted to do the same for countless others. King had a big heart—and a busy life.

The Problem of Busyness

In 1957, two years into the movement sparked by Rosa Parks's refusal to surrender her bus seat to a white person, Walter McCall, a Morehouse and Crozer classmate, mailed King some timely pastoral advice: "Seek to be alone, leave the scene, seek solace from above as this will do much to keep your parts in-tact, revitalized, well re-energized and—daring[ly] fortified for the great tasks at hand and those that lie ahead."[4]

McCall noted that even Jesus had left the scene. Like McCall, King would have known that the gospels of the New Testament include stories of Jesus pulling away from crowds on numerous occasions so that he could journey toward a place of quiet rest and experience the one he called "Abba." The gospel of Mark records a story of Jesus retreating, with just a handful of disciples, to a mountain far away from the crowds. It was during this mountaintop retreat, according to Mark, that God transfigured Jesus and addressed him as "my beloved son."[5]

McCall's message did not fall on entirely deaf ears. As his work increasingly consumed his schedule, King became deeply aware of his personal need to retreat from the pressing crowds and trek to the serenity of the mountains. Consider his reply to an interviewer who asked him in 1965, eight years after McCall's letter, how he would spend a week with no interruptions:

---

[3]Ibid., 137.

[4]In "From Walter McCall," *Symbol of the Movement, January 1957–December 1958,* vol. 4 of *The Papers of Martin Luther King, Jr.,* ed. Clayborne Carson et al. (Berkeley: University of California Press, 2000), 137.

[5]See Mark 9:2–3, 7.

It's difficult to imagine such a thing, but if I had the luxury of an entire week, I would spend it meditating and reading, refreshing myself spiritually and intellectually…Amidst the struggle, amidst the frustrations, amidst the endless work, I often reflect that I am forever *giving*—never pausing to take in. I feel urgently the need for even an hour of time to get away, to withdraw, to refuel.[6]

King had expressed the same sentiment many times before 1965. Just after his farewell address at Dexter Avenue Baptist Church, for example, he laid out his personal struggle at an MIA mass meeting: "What I have been doing is giving, giving, giving, and not stopping to retreat and meditate like I should. If the situation is not changed, I will be a physical and psychological wreck. I have to reorganize my personality and reorient my life."[7]

Looking back on his Montgomery days at yet another point, King bemoaned the lack of time he had given to deliberate, sustained reflection. "I felt terribly frustrated," he stated, "over my inability to retreat, concentrate, and reflect." The frustration, according to King, was compounded by his sacrificial actions: "My whole life seemed to be centered around giving something out and only rarely taking something in."

Therein, of course, lay the grave danger—by not taking time to reflect, by not taking time for himself, he had begun to deplete the resources, physical and spiritual, that he required for survival as an individual and as the leader of the movement. "My failure to reflect," he wrote, "would do harm not only to me as a person, but to the total movement."[8]

Burdened by a crowded schedule, King came to realize that we cannot even begin to reflect when we are busy, busy, busy, no matter how important the busyness may be, and that when we cannot reflect, we lose a sense of, among other things, the meaning and purpose of our lives. That is exactly the way he felt in the 1965 interview mentioned above, when he told the interviewer that he needed

---

[6]Martin Luther King Jr., "*Playboy* Interview," *A Testament of Hope: The Essential Writings of Martin Luther King, Jr.,* ed. James M. Washington (San Francisco: Harper SanFrancisco, 1986), 372.

[7]Quoted in Garrow, *Bearing the Cross*, 125.

[8]King, *Autobiography*, 137.

time just to think: "I need more time to think through what is being done, to take time out from the mechanics of the movement, to reflect on the *meaning* of the movement."[9]

Though he often thrived on nonstop creative action among crowds of people, King knew that when we are marching toward the beloved community every day, we may lose sight of the reason we began to take the first step; that when we are on the road day in and day out, we may lose touch with those who remain at home; that when crowds surround us all the time, we may forget who we are and whom we belong to; and that when we are forever giving to others, we may end up with nothing left to give. In other words, King knew the cruel irony that our commitment to nonstop creative action may actually end up destroying our own lives.

King experienced the destructive potential of busyness especially when life was not going so well for him. Andrew Young has noted that King grew tired, even depressed, when he and the movement seemed to lack direction and when results in particular marches and movements were not especially favorable. At these points, King would complain of being busy, way too busy, and then he would just collapse in exhaustion, deeply aware that creative living sometimes requires withdrawing, right here and now, from the incessant demands of an overbooked schedule, even one that he had insisted on at an earlier point, when the days seemed long and the nights short.

The Point of Retreating

During those moments of intense disappointment and exhaustion, King believed that retreating to the mountain would help turn his life around. It would allow him to carve out a space where others could not grab at him, seeking to take everything that he himself needed to survive as an individual. More positively stated, it would help him receive from others, especially God, the resources he needed to keep on keeping on.

And this gets to the purpose of retreating. For King, the essential purpose of retreating is not simply to desert the crowds, or our community, family, and workplace. The practice of retreating is not an end in itself, but only a means to an end—a means by which we,

---

[9]King, "*Playboy* Interview," *Testament*, 372.

with the help of others, can refuel ourselves so that we will have enough energy to create both a healthy personal life and the beloved community that God intends for everyone.

Creative living, in King's thought, thus requires retreating from the demands of creative doing, but only with the purpose of receiving what we need in order to return to a life of creative action. If we are going to retreat to the mountain, in other words, we must make sure that we come back down to the valley, where our action is required to overturn obstructions to the beloved community. If we are going to *be* on the mountaintop, we must be there only so that we can *do* the will of God in the valley.

A Time for Silence

When we picture King, we most likely imagine him leading yet another march, or standing before a microphone, in front of a crowd of people, and delivering a passionate sermon or speech. Although that is an accurate picture of the public King, it certainly does not represent the whole King, especially the part that sought to retreat from a life of sheer busyness. Indeed, far away from the crowds, with their noisy, incessant demands, King was a man who embraced silence as a practice of creative living.

King turned to silence because of his belief that we cannot hear our own voices, let alone the voice of God, when we are speaking all the time, or when others are shouting at us all the time—that sometimes we need to keep our mouths shut, or shut out the words of others, so that we can hear the voice of guidance and wisdom deep inside us.

After he returned from a trip to India, King sought to make room in his schedule for an entire day of silence every week—a whole day of silent meditation.[10] Although his efforts to take an entire day were only partly successful, King remained committed, throughout the rest of his life, to creating moments of sheer silence, with the hope of discerning the call of love that he might otherwise miss in the shouts of the crowd. Love, King believed, sometimes comes to us in the quietest of ways.

---

[10]King, *Autobiography*, 137.

Know Thyself

King took the occasion of silence to delve deeply into the chambers of his own heart and meditate on the purpose and direction of his life. He sketched this meditative practice in the 1965 interview:

> I subject myself to endless self-purification and to endless self-analysis. I question and soul-search constantly into myself to be as certain as I can that I am fulfilling the true meaning of my work, that I am maintaining my sense of purpose, that I am holding fast to my ideals, that I am guiding my people in the right direction.[11]

These personal words clearly reveal King's vision of creative living in moments of silence: Silence is for deliberate self-reflection, a practice he understood, in many ways, as a matter of life and death. In King's view, when we do not take time to reflect on ourselves— on the people we have become—we lose a sense of our reason for being: We become purposeless, directionless, downright lost. But when we do make time to reflect, we can actually discern whether or not we are true to the meaning and proper direction of life. Through deliberate self-reflection we can prioritize the claims on our lives, reorganize our personalities, and reorient our full lives, making sure that their disparate parts are brought under the unified purpose of serving the will of God, come what may.

Interestingly, King believed that self-analysis was also a necessary practice for anyone experiencing personal or social problems of any sort, and so he recommended the practice numerous times in his column for *Ebony*. For example, in reply to a husband who wondered how to respond to his wife, who evidently showed no interest in their marriage, King wrote: "In advising anyone on marital problems I usually begin by urging each person to do an honest job of self analysis. Although you feel that you have done all in your power to make the marriage a success it would be well to ask yourself the question whether you have done anything to cause your wife to react the way she does."[12]

---

[11]King, "*Playboy* Interview," *Testament*, 376.
[12]King, "Advice for Living," *Papers*, 4: 348.

King also recommended self-analysis for a young woman wondering how she could make her negligent mother love her,[13] a wife inquiring how she should respond to her husband's ridicule,[14] and a woman whose husband was having an affair. Encouraging the jilted woman to practice self-analysis, King even supplied the questions for her: "Do you spend too much time with the children and the house and not pay attention to him? Are you careful with your grooming? Do you nag? Do you make him feel important...like somebody?"[15]

In reply to a twenty-four-year-old female who had never had a "steady boy friend," and wanted to know what she could do "to find a nice young man," King recommended that she too begin with self-analysis: "One of the first things you should do in an attempt to get at your problem is to go through a process of self-examination. Are you sure that you have a radiating personality, a pleasant disposition, and that feminine charm which every man admires?"[16] King suggested the same practice, with adjusted questions, for a man desirous of "meeting nice women."[17]

Unfortunately, King did not seem to have any sense that these questions might have placed the burden of proof on the wrong person. The questions he supplied for the woman whose husband was having an affair, for example, seem to place the burden, unfairly, on the wronged woman. Still, if nothing else, this lack of sensitivity is a clear indicator that King strongly believed that a key practice of creative living is to create time and space for us to enter into the deepest recesses of our heart and explore every dimension of our identities: our personalities, our bodies, our motives for living the way we do, our life practices, and our relationships with others. For King, silent moments are for entering the depths of our existence and discerning who we really are and who we should be. Doing so, in King's view, can help us understand not only who we are but also some of the reasons underlying people's reactions to us. In addition, self-analysis will prevent us from entering into situations that are

---

[13]King, "Advice for Living," *Papers*, 4: 401.
[14]Ibid., 541.
[15]Ibid., 459.
[16]Ibid., 504.
[17]Ibid., 418.

not true to our core selves as well as aid us in extracting ourselves from situations that harm the persons we should be.

Know Thyself with Others

Still, for King, creative self-analysis does not mean a stereoscopic focus on merely our own individual personalities. King believed that, because we live in community, self-reflection should always entail reflection on others. Because we are not islands unto ourselves, because what affects us affects others, and because what affects others affects us, thinking of ourselves as somehow separate from others is nothing less than an exercise in futility.

When he told the interviewer that he desired time to reflect on the meaning of the *movement*, then, King partly meant that he needed time to understand his individual leadership in light of others. As an insightful political strategist, King understood that his leadership could not take its proper shape, let alone move ahead with confidence, until he made time to reflect on both his dedicated followers (their attitudes and abilities) as well as his vicious enemies (their intentions, designs, and power). Knowing that a failure to reflect on others could easily undermine his own tactical strategy in pulling the movement forward, King firmly held that time is for deliberately stepping back and reflecting on the people around us. The community, in his view, can often make or break the effectiveness of individual witness to the beloved community.

Turn to God in Prayer

But King certainly had something else in mind, too, when he spoke of the need to reflect on the *meaning* of the movement: He had in mind the presence of God, the ultimate source of the meaning of our lives. True to his vocation as a black Baptist preacher, King believed that we can understand ourselves fully—our identities, purpose, and direction—only by discerning, listening to, and heeding the presence of God in our lives.

Time on the mountain is thus not only for self-analysis; it is also for intentionally reflecting on the Creator of the mountain. Time is for studying and hearing the word of God through the prophets of old, experiencing the power of the love of God in the life and death of Jesus of Nazareth, and encountering the Spirit of truth within us. Time on the mountain is for opening ourselves to being named, and claimed, by the God who comforts and challenges us—*Martin Luther, stand up for righteousness!*

Yet again, remember the kitchen experience, when King heard the voice of Jesus telling him to stand up for righteousness, to stand up for justice, to stand up for truth. In his witness to that story, King was clearly implying that, unless we make time to sit alone at midnight and begin a conversation with the God of midnight, we will never hear what the Spirit of Jesus can tell us about the dawning of a new day. Unless we retreat from the crowds and surrender ourselves to the Spirit, we will never experience the opportunity for the transfiguration of our own characters. Unless we head to the mountain and bow our heads in a quest for the power that can make a way out of no way, we will never sense the Spirit blowing down old structures, clearing the way for our new efforts to create the beloved community. For King, prayer is an indispensable part of our spiritual journey on the mountain.

To be sure, King was a bit wary of many people who turned to prayer, especially those who focused on prayer on the mountain to the exclusion of down-and-dirty work in the valley.[18] In fact, though he prayed faithfully, King understood prayer to be wholly insufficient for the march toward the beloved community. As he put it, "God, who gave us minds for thinking and bodies for working, would defeat his own purpose if he permitted us to obtain through prayer what may come through hard work and intelligence. Prayer is a marvelous and necessary supplement of our feeble efforts, but it is a dangerous substitute."[19]

Still, King found prayer to be a necessary ingredient of creative living. Through prayer we encounter the source of being, love, justice, and power, each of which is required for life in the beloved community. By talking with and listening to God, we come face-to-face, right here and right now, with the reason for our existence

---

[18]King critiqued President Johnson's proposal for a Day of Prayer in response to inner-city riots exactly on this point. "As a minister," King stated, "I take prayer too seriously to use it as an excuse for avoiding work and responsibility," in Martin Luther King Jr., "Nonviolence and Social Change," *The Trumpet of Conscience* (San Francisco: Harper and Row, 1976), 59.

[19]King, "The Answer to a Perplexing Question," *Strength to Love* (Philadelphia: Fortress Press, 1981), 131–32.

and the source of strength for life in the valley. Prayer gives us courage and comfort: It is only in prayer, after all, when we can hear the voice within that says, "Stand up for truth! Stand up for righteousness! And lo, I will always be with you, even until the end of the age."

In King's view, we should withdraw to the mountain and pray for ourselves—for strength, optimism, the power of love, right vision, broad understanding, abiding faith, and the courage to be and do. And we should pray for others, especially our enemies—for a change of mind, a change of plans, a new understanding.[20]

For King, it is also important for us to withdraw in prayer not only at regularly scheduled times, like before meals or bedtime, but especially when there is no time to pray: We should go to the mountain in prayer just when we think we cannot get there. King did exactly that just before he spoke at the first MIA meeting in Montgomery. With twenty minutes to prepare the speech, and with the minutes passing by fast, he did not dig into the mechanics of writing a speech, or call upon his advisers to gather around him with sage advice. He prayed. "With nothing left but faith in a power whose matchless strength stands over against the frailties and inadequacies of human nature," King testified, "I turned to God in prayer. My words were brief and simple, asking God to restore my balance and to be with me in a time when I needed His guidance more than ever."[21]

Just when we believe that we have no time, then, the time has come for us to retreat to the mountain, pray, feel the assurance of divine presence, and discern the course of our present lives. King firmly believed that God will hear and answer our prayers. Again, King believed that God is personal, and so he held that when we retreat to the mountain, we should just expect to encounter a God who already knows us by name, a God who can help direct us in the details of our lives, a God who already knows what is in our hearts.

King also believed he heard the voice of God in many ways. To be sure, he thought he heard it in the cries of the hungry, the thirsty, the imprisoned, the naked, and the homeless, but he also felt that he heard it with great clarity in the quiet of the hour, at a kitchen table

---

[20]See King, "Who Speaks for the South?" *Testament*, 92; King, *Papers*, 4: 370.
[21]King, *Autobiography*, 58.

well beyond midnight, when he was alone, silent, delving into the inner chambers of his heart, where he trusted a personal God would speak and show him a way out of no way. Trusting that he would hear the voice of a personal God, King turned to prayer throughout his public career, especially during intensely difficult moments, like the time he struggled with his own response to the Vietnam War. King agonized over his response so much that he withdrew to the mountain to devote sustained periods of thought and prayer about the proper course for his words and deeds. It literally took him months to decide which way to go, but King believed the result was worth the time. After returning to the valley, he looked back to the mountain and reported on hearing the internal voice yet again: "Something said to me, 'Martin, you have got to stand up on this. No matter what it means.'"[22]

For King, then, time is for listening in silence for the voice of God within us. God speaks, and if we retreat to the mountain, practicing the discipline of silence, and listening to the voice within us, we will hear what God has to say: Stand up and create the beloved community!

Take Time to Read

God, according to King, is not the only one who speaks in moments of solitude and silence on the mountain—other people do, too. King often entered into silent conversations with others who had traveled to the mountain long before he arrived there, including the saints of his past and, more importantly here, authors of great books of all kinds, especially philosophy and theology. As a reading of his pilgrimage to nonviolence will suggest, King was deeply familiar with many of the so-called "great books" of Western civilization, classic and modern.[23] And he often craved time to read so that his own reflections might enjoy greater depth. In a 1965 interview, King said that if he had the luxury of an entire week with no interruptions, he would spend it not only meditating but also *reading.*

---

[22]King, *Autobiography*, 335.
[23]Martin Luther King Jr., *Stride Toward Freedom: The Montgomery Story* (New York: Harper & Row, 1958), 90–107.

As King understood it, time on the mountain is for the practice of reading so that we can refresh ourselves not only emotionally and spiritually but also *intellectually*. Simply stated, our calling in life is to read—and to make sense of our reflections in light of the expressions of the best minds available in print. King believed that because God has given us a precious mind to use, we had better use it by stretching it—reading the best of books. Indeed, King often faulted clergy, as well as other professionals, for failing to study the new theories and methods in their fields.

So when we go to the mountain, we must be sure to pick up a book and read the thoughts of those who have already been there. We need not reinvent the wheel; we just need to read the great books already available to us and creatively adapt the wisdom of others for our own work in creating the beloved community. In this sense, creative living is *inspired* living.

Prepare to Share

Though intensely personal, a mountain experience is not for us to store deep in our hearts, where no one can discover it. In King's view, God intends for us to share our experience with others, and so before we leave the mountain we should also sit down and interpret the experience as clearly as possible so that others can benefit from it as we march together toward the beloved community.

Believing that creative living is ultimately outward-focused, King interpreted his own time on the mountain by writing long letters (for example, *A Letter from Birmingham City Jail*); developing strategic plans; and preparing sermons, speeches, and prayers—reflections on personal character and social justice that King intended for public consumption.[24] Yes, many of them were products of King's own

---

[24]King was not a contemplative type who kept his spiritual thoughts to himself; he was a preacher who sought to share his social vision as widely as possible so that others could help him create the beloved community. For more on this theme, see Frederick L. Downing, "Martin Luther King, Jr., as Public Theologian," *Theology Today* 44 (April 1987). See also Christopher Beem, "American Liberalism and the Christian Church: Stanley Hauerwas vs. Martin Luther King, Jr.," *Journal of Religious Ethics* 23 (Spring 1995): 117–64. "King's ministry," Beem argues, "was thoroughly public, intimately associated with the political structure, and grounded in his Christian conviction that Christian values and those professed by American liberalism overlap" (123).

unique experience on the mountaintop, far away from the crowds of people, but he offered them for all of the people, hoping that we would benefit from them in our own efforts to live creatively. Even in solitude, then, creative living is living for others.

Time for Family

King understood time on the mountain to be not only for reflection in solitude and silence, but also for enjoying the company of family and friends. The practice of retreating, he believed, need not translate into the life of a religious hermit. As King understood it, retreating provides both the occasion for solo reflection and the opportunity to be with our loved ones, especially the people who stick with us through it all, refreshing our personalities and strengthening us for work in the valley.

It is no secret that King struggled with the demands of family life. When asked in the 1965 *Playboy* interview about his own family, King was bluntly honest. No, he said, he did not have much time for them at all. On average, he was home no more than two days a week, and sometimes he was gone for two or three weeks at a time. But King added that every day he was at home, he would try to spend a few hours with his children. "And on Tuesdays when I'm not out of town, I don't go to the office. I keep this for my quiet day of reading and silence and meditation, and an entire evening with Mrs. King and the children."[25]

King regretted the time he spent away from his family, finding it to be "one of the frustrating aspects" of his role as leader of the civil rights movement. "It's just impossible," he confessed, "to carry out the responsibilities of a father and husband when you have these kinds of demands."[26]

King was so troubled because he sensed that he *should* have been a present father and husband, and with this unspoken imperative in mind, he counseled others to do what he himself was not doing. For example, when offering advice in *Ebony* to a traveling entertainer whose wife wanted him to take a more secure job, King stated: "I can see how your wife would be desirous of your spending more

[25]King, "*Playboy* Interview," *Testament*, 372.
[26]King, *Autobiography*, 39.

time with the family and certainly you should seek to arrange your working schedule so that it will be possible to devote more time to your home life."[27]

On the other hand, King conceded to the entertainer that it sometimes takes considerable time to get established in one's profession—time away from the family. Indeed, King himself took time—a lot of it—to establish his work as a civil rights leader. In terms of time allotment alone, he often sacrificed his family, leaving them far behind in his quest to strengthen the movement. David Garrow has reported that, when reflecting on the conflict of duties between his role as family man and his role as civil rights leader, King would even sometimes say, "A man who devotes himself to a cause, who dedicates himself to a cause doesn't need a family."[28]

This does not mean, of course, that King did not love his family, nor does it mean that he would ever leave them. If we take time to look at his face in the pictures of him with his children, we can easily begin to understand that some of his best moments away from the crowds must have been the times he spent with his family on the mountain. No matter how much he let his professional schedule spiral out of control, it seems that he treasured the time he made for them. King even went to great lengths to bring the movement to his family, so much so that Dexter Scott King remembers his father's close coworkers in the movement as his own uncles and aunts:

> I never knew a man with so many brothers and sisters as my father—and resulting aunts and uncles for me and my brother and sisters. Not only was there Uncle A.D. and Aunt Naomi, or Aunt Christine and Uncle Isaac, our own blood relatives and his in-laws, there was also Uncle Andy, Uncle Ralph, Uncle Harry, Uncle Bob, Uncle Junius. Uncle Ralph was Ralph Abernathy. Uncle Andy was Andrew Young. Uncle Harry was Harry Belafonte. Uncle Junius was Junius Griffin.

---

[27]King, "Advice for Living," *Papers* 4: 394. This section helps to show that King did not always follow the advice he dispensed to others. Michael Jinkins, in "An Apologia for the Theological Exercise of Power in Christian Ministry," *Journal of Pastoral Theology* 7 (Summer 1997), 126, is wrong when he argues the following without qualification: "King's rhetoric leads King himself into a progressively deeper commitment. Thus, as he led others to act, he acted himself."

[28]Garrow, *Bearing the Cross*, 115.

Uncle Bob was either Robert Green or Robert Johnson. Everybody was related, even if not by blood. And if anybody got in trouble, my family showed up to support him or her, because that was our habit.[29]

On a related note, it has been widely observed that King's relationship with his wife, Coretta, suffered in some ways during his years as leader of the movement. Indeed, the charges of a struggling marriage seem to increase with each passing year, though Ralph Abernathy's autobiography, with its allegation that King was romantically linked with several women on the night before his death, was a culmination of stories on King's alleged womanizing.[30]

To be sure, the marriage experienced some strain, in large part because of King's deliberate decision to sacrifice his family, including his relationship with Coretta, for the movement. Yet, even deep into the marriage, he offered the kindest of words about Coretta, describing her as helpful, consoling, courageous, and understanding.[31] "I am convinced," he stated, "that if I had not had a wife with the fortitude, strength, and calmness of Corrie, I could not have withstood the ordeals and tensions surrounding the movement."[32]

---

[29]Dexter Scott King, *Growing Up King: An Intimate Memoir* (New York: Warner Books, 2003), 23.

[30]Ralph David Abernathy, *And the Walls Came Tumbling Down* (New York: Harper & Row, 1989), 434–37. For a pointed critique of Abernathy's allegations, see James Wall, "Abernathy Takes a Cheap Shot," *Christian Century* 106 (November 1, 1989): 971–72. "Kissing and telling," Wall wrote, "is never a gracious thing to do…There is an even greater lack of graciousness when the telling is done not by the kisser or the kissee but by a voyeur." King himself addressed themes of marriage and sex in, among other places, a reply to a female *Ebony* reader who questioned him about the morality of premarital sex: "I think you should hold firm to the principle of premarital virginity. The problems created by premarital sex relationships are far greater than the problems created by premarital virginity. The suspicions, fears, and guilt feelings generated by premarital sex relations are contributing factors to the present breakdown of the family." See King, "Advice for Living," *Papers*, 4: 306 for the text of his complete answer. For an insightful reflection on King's attitudes toward sex, as well as his sexual behavior, see Michael Eric Dyson, *I May Not Get There with You: The True Martin Luther King, Jr.* (New York: The Free Press, 2000), 155–74. Especially insightful is Dyson's understanding of King's moral character in light of the allegations of his womanizing.

[31]King, *Autobiography*, 38–39.

[32]Ibid., 37.

To the last, King felt internal conflict regarding the time he spent away from Coretta and the children, and he felt so because he truly believed that time is not just for marching in the movement, but also for relaxing with one's family—eating delicious food with them, praying with them, sharing devotions and worshiping with them, playing with them, listening to music with them, and falling asleep with them.[33]

King's internal struggle makes most sense when considered in light of the close-knit family he enjoyed as a child. His childhood family was *the* source of refuge and strength for him, especially when the reality of segregation began to crash into his life. Although he was surrounded by a system of hatred, King grew up in a loving environment that enjoyed an intact family—a grandmother who doted on him, a mother who taught him that he was "somebody," and a father who showed him that men could love.

The power of this memory never left him, and it gave substance to what he wanted to live out in many ways—the life of a man who could leave the crowds behind and find a family gathered around him in love. Yes, he struggled mightily with the family he created, but to the end King wanted his children to sense his belief that time is for gathering family on the mountain and passing on the love that only strong families can share. In fact, this lesson is what Dexter King remembers his father embodying so well: "He sought refuge in his children, his family. He became us."[34]

Because he found family time to be key to his own creative actions, and because he truly believed in the redemptive power of a

---

[33]King wrote on music in particular in his *Ebony* column (King, "Advice for Living," *Papers*, 4: 392). In reply to a young musician inquiring whether it would be sinful for him to play rock music for a living, King wrote: "It seems to me that one must decide to either play gospel music or rock and roll. The two are totally incompatible. The profound sacred and spiritual meaning of the great music of the church must never be mixed with the transitory quality of rock and roll music. The former serves to lift men's souls to higher levels of reality, and therefore to God; the latter so often plunges men's minds into degrading and immoral depths." Interestingly, King's son Dexter became a huge fan of rock and roll. Equally interesting, Dexter reports that, though King preferred gospel music, "He often tapped his foot and bobbed his head to secular music, and he didn't deny it to us—he couldn't, not in Vine City. Music was everywhere," in Dexter Scott King, *Growing Up King*, 12.

[34]Dexter Scott King, *Growing Up King*, 23.

family life based on love, King encouraged families to stay together whenever possible. This type of encouragement appeared several times in his *Ebony* column, including his reply to a reader who, frustrated with the intense animosity between her husband and her daughter from a previous marriage, asked if she should divorce her husband:

> I do not think that a divorce is the answer to your problem. It would only create new and more complicated problems, especially with reference to your own personal adjustment. A better approach to the problem would be to seek to bring about a degree of understanding between your daughter and your husband. People fail to get along with each other because they fear each other. They fear each other because they do not know each other. They don't know each other because they have not properly communicated with each other. This is probably the case with your daughter and husband. They have probably never known each other nor properly communicated with each other. If you can bring them together and urge them to honestly discuss their differences and confess their mistakes, wherever they have been made, this, I believe, will go a long, long way toward restoring a broken relationship.[35]

This reply gets to the heart of King's own practice of spending time with his family—communication. According to King, if we are to spend creative time with our families, and if our families are to stay together, we must show a willingness to sit down and communicate openly with our loved ones, letting them know our innermost thoughts and feelings, even if our loved ones intensely disagree with us. Successful communication, in King's thought, makes or breaks not only political and economic negotiations with power brokers, but also the dynamics of a family. This is why King made a deliberate effort to refrain from spanking his children, choosing instead the practice of open communication—a practice that Dexter Scott King describes beautifully in a reflection on the way his father talked him out of playing with toy guns:

---

[35]King, "Advice for Living," *Papers*, 4: 401.

The way he spoke was so effective that at the end of it he actually had us destroy those plastic guns...I liked the toy guns, and the real guns police and security officers wore. But I was moved by what my father had said. He had such a cool way of explaining things that it was almost like we were happy to do what he had asked us to do, even though I still didn't quite know why.

This and other lessons stuck with me. He was very much a talker, he would talk about subjects with us, was intimate in his feelings, in terms of our being able to understand the subject and his feelings. You felt like his equal, almost, like he was bringing you up in the world to his level, not like he was coming down to you. He was soothing to listen to, authoritative you knew, because he was Daddy, but also deliberate, precise; when he spoke, you listened.[36]

For King, this is what time on the mountain is for—open communication with our families so that together we can avoid the obstructions before us and continue our march toward the beloved community. Families that communicate openly, in King's thought, are the keystone of the type of creative action that builds communities of love, justice, and peace.

Time for Friends

King also believed that time on the mountain is for creating and sustaining the practice of friendship. Indeed, he loved to leave the crowds behind and head to the mountain with a small circle of men and women who truly let him be Martin Luther King Jr., the whole man. For King, this is also what mountain time is especially for—open sharing with our best friends so that we can be our whole selves.

He did exactly that with Ralph David Abernathy, the closest of his personal friends, who was with King from the beginning of the Montgomery movement until the day he died in Memphis. With Abernathy, King could pray and share devotions, tell jokes and mimic the enemy, smoke cigarettes and drink more than milk, and even

---

[36]Dexter Scott King, *Growing Up King*, 35–36.

share his deepest sexual secrets. With Abernathy, that is, King could be himself.

King clearly believed that Abernathy was the best of friends—someone who would love him and stick by him even when learning the most private details of his life. And Abernathy, in turn, felt the same about King—that he was a true friend who stuck by him through it all. Clearly, in Abernathy, among others, King discovered that friends are the ones we can open our hearts to with trust. They are the men and women who provide us with the time and space we need in private to refuel for the incessant demands of public life. They are our lifelines on the deadly march toward the promised land. Friends are the stuff of creative living and loving.

According to the accounts of his closest associates, King was an easy friend—like a "big kid," fun-loving, ever ready to chat throughout the night or eat another plate of food, and often willing to carry the burden of friendship.[37] He was also an empowering friend. It was his best friend Abernathy whom King turned to when he could not carry out his public responsibilities because of illness, fatigue, or scheduling conflicts. It was Abernathy whom he looked for when his private life became too messy to handle himself. And it was Abernathy whom he envisioned as carrying the mantle after his death. Through his friendship with Abernathy, King expressed his conviction that time on the mountain is not only for gaining strength from our friends in private moments alone with them, but also for trusting them to go into the valley and carry out the creative work that we have only begun to do.

Time to Be Acted Upon

King's heavy reliance on family and friends suggests that he was far from someone who saw himself as the one and only actor in the

---

[37]On the last day of his life, King grabbed Andrew Young as he walked into King's room at the Gaston Hotel, threw him on the bed, and started to beat him with a pillow, asking him why he did not report to him, King, earlier. Young characterized the fun-loving King in that moment as acting "like a big kid." See his interviews in *Eyes on the Prize II: America at the Racial Crossroads—1965 to 1985*, no. 3, *The Promised Land (1967–1968)*, Blackside, Inc., Boston, 1989 (videocassette). In the same video, Coretta Scott King, in typical understated fashion, offered this comment on King and food: "Martin, of course, liked to eat."

universe: King was no soloist. In fact, he often downplayed the importance of his own role, describing it in uncharacteristically passive terms:

> One of the prayers that I prayed to God every day was: "Oh God, help me to see myself in true perspective. Help me, oh God, to see that I'm just a symbol of the movement. Help me to see that I'm a victim of what the Germans call a *Zeitgeist* and that something was getting ready to happen in history. And that a boycott would have taken place in Montgomery, Alabama, if I had never come to Alabama. Help me to realize that I'm where I am because of the forces of history and because of the fifty thousand Negroes of Alabama who will never get their names in the papers and in the headlines. Oh, God, help me to see that where I stand today, I stand because others helped me to stand there and because the forces of history projected me there."[38]

Even a quick read of his acceptance speech at the awarding of the Nobel Peace Prize reveals that King attributed much of his success to others—friends, family, acquaintances, and strangers who selected him as their representative.[39] In addition, King was certain that there was a spirit of freedom manifesting itself in history—infusing people, realizing itself through them, and carrying them toward the promised land. It was not just any spirit that did this; for King, the liberating spirit of the times was nothing less than the Spirit of God.

King maintained that this *Zeitgeist* had acted upon him in Montgomery; it had swept him up and projected him into the movement for freedom. He truly believed that he was who he was, not only because of his own skills and intelligence, but primarily because the *Zeitgeist* had infused him, sweeping him into the fight for civil rights. It was not Martin Luther King Jr. who had grabbed the reigns of leadership; the *Zeitgeist* had thrust the reigns into his hands in a kairotic moment.[40] King even went so far as to say: "You

---

[38]King, *Autobiography*, 105.

[39]King, *Autobiography*, 257.

[40]King depicted the role of Rosa Parks in the same way: "She was a victim of both the forces of history and the forces of destiny. She had been tracked down by the *Zeitgeist*—the spirit of the time," in King, *Stride Toward Freedom*, 44.

know there comes a time when time itself is ready for change. The time has come in Montgomery, and I had nothing to do with it."[41]

Though this view has its own problems in terms of personal responsibility and accountability, it served King well in recognizing that his unique, particular actions could never begin to describe and reveal the whole story of his life. Yes, King recognized that he acted as few others had, but he also believed that he was acted upon as few others had been. Believing this, he tried to assume the role of a humble servant and to call upon others to do the same.[42]

For King, then, we can act incessantly, but if we are acting against the Spirit of the times, our actions are futile, worthless, and ineffective. What we must first do is simply *be*—be open to the Spirit of the times. We must never stand against the Spirit, trying to make our own mark, but rather allow it to roll right into our spirit. If we allow it to act upon us, the *Zeitgeist* will sweep us to where we need to be and do.

In this sense, King's vision of creative living requires the practice of allowing the Spirit to act upon us so that we can understand which actions we must undertake. Creative action thus presupposes being—being in discernment. For King, we can discern the *Zeitgeist* in the direction of the crowds surrounding us, but we can never really discern the will of the *Zeitgeist* for us until we withdraw from the crowds and feel the wind blowing through us. And so we must go to the mountaintop and *feel* the Spirit of the times filling us up and sweeping us forward. That is what creative living is about—allowing the Spirit to act upon us before we act for it.

Time to Wait

King's trips to the mountain suggest that he recognized the fundamental importance of waiting. To be sure, he stood firmly against

[41]King, *Autobiography*, 78.

[42]According to Stanley Levison, King's sense of being swept up by the Spirit of the time left him with the belief that he did not really deserve the acclaim that came his way. Consequently, King tried to dissociate himself from the material benefits that came his way. As Levison put it to Garrow, "He always thought of ways he could somehow live up to it [the acclaim], and he often talked about taking a vow of poverty: getting rid of everything he owned—including his house—so that he could at least feel that nothing material came to him from his efforts." Garrow, *Bearing the Cross*, 588.

passively waiting in a state of purposeless inactivity, but King fully affirmed the spiritual practice of waiting for the right time.

Andrew Young has reported that, when King was unsure about which direction to head in, or when he was anxious about his actions, he would pretend to be sick and head to the hospital for a check-up. These hospital visits may sound a bit peculiar, even like an attention-grabbing ploy, but they actually played a key role in King's life: They provided him with time to wait for the next step. They gave him the time he needed to wait for the wisdom that comes through personal reflection, for the renewed energy that comes through close contact with loved ones, for the direction that comes through the movement of the Spirit. In the hospital, among other places, King could simply wait.

Although he was not always patient, at least in terms of the progress of the movement, the hospital patient King acknowledged that sometimes we cannot do what we want and need to do. Sometimes there are not enough people to form a strong resistance; at other times the oppressors have so much power they can knock us down before we even arrive in town for the march; and at still other times we just lack the resources, spiritual and material, to discern where we must go.

In this sense, King understood that creative living is not just something we create at will; it is also something that we must wait for. Sometimes, that is, we cannot begin to live creatively until we wait for the arrival of the key ingredients for creative living. Yes, we can and should hurry along their arrival as much as we can, but we would also do well to remember that we are not God: We can do only what we can do, and sometimes what we can do is not sufficient for moving ahead.

King thus believed that when we can act no more, the best we can do is to wait. Go to the mountain, reflecting, sharing, opening ourselves to the Spirit of the times, and praying that the Spirit will show us the way out of no way. This type of waiting, King believed, is not escapism; it is just plain and simple trust. Faithful waiting trusts that, when we do not know which way to go, the best we can do is to be—to pull back and wait for the Spirit to sweep us up yet again. For King, that is what the Spirit does—the Spirit always empowers us in moments of waiting to regroup our personalities, reorient our lives, and see a way we never saw before. God, after all, is able.

Coda: Return to the Valley

King often confessed a temptation to stay on the mountaintop—to retreat to a lifetime of reflection and meditation. When asked in 1965 whether or not he would devote the rest of his life to the cause, he said: "If need be, yes. But I dream of the day when the demands cast upon me will be greatly diminished."[43] He dreamed of teaching in a university, assuming a major pulpit, just getting away from the nonstop demands of the movement.[44]

Yet he never made any real step in that direction. In the deepest recesses of his heart, King felt that the Spirit had swept him into the valley, and that he belonged there. "But something within me," he said in 1965, "reminds me that the valley calls me in spite of its agonies, dangers, and frustrating moments. I must return to the valley."[45]

Not only did King refuse to take any steps toward pulling out of the movement; he also had a difficult time getting away for even short periods. Indeed, it seems fair to suggest that he never took enough time to withdraw. Sure, he would schedule days for silence and reflection, but he would often let people barge into them. He would take sabbaticals and vacations here and there, but even then he would let others interrupt with the business of the movement.

King's difficulty with pulling back from the movement is quite understandable in light of his own beliefs and practices. It is not easy to take a break when one preaches the urgency of *now*. It is not easy to go on vacation when one states, without qualification, that there should be no rest on the march toward the beloved community. It is not easy to withdraw when one's success makes others clamor for even greater success.

As noted in the beginning of this chapter, King recognized that his ministry suffered because of his busyness. Coretta certainly thought

[43]King, "*Playboy* Interview," *Testament*, 375.

[44]See Garrow, *Bearing the Cross*, 603. King even proposed taking a whole year off just for the purpose of reflection.

[45]King, *Autobiography*, 264. King also knew that the crowds loved him and that he loved them. Garrow, *Bearing the Cross*, 603, reports that King liked to walk to a restaurant for lunch on Auburn Avenue, and that it would often take him an hour to walk the one-and-a-half block stretch, just because he loved mixing with the people and would make it a point to take time to speak with anyone desirous of his attention.

that, once he became committed to the movement, his sermons suffered; he no longer had the required time to plan and prepare for them, write them out, and commit them to memory.[46] Others believe that the serious time constraints also affected his work as president of the Montgomery Improvement Association, as well as his leadership of the Southern Christian Leadership Conference.

King would simply let his schedule spiral out of control to the point where he felt that he was doing lots of things but none of them very well, including personal care. But he would just keep going anyway, most times until he collapsed in periods of depression and exhaustion. Obviously, King knew in those tough times that that was not creative living at its best. Unfortunately, though, he never journeyed up the mountain as far as he needed to for refueling, and at the tender age of 38, he was murdered during one of those painful, unnecessary states of depression and exhaustion.[47] Ever giving, King had his life taken away.

---

[46]Garrow, *Bearing the Cross*, 122.

[47]Here I am reminded of a simple yet beautiful sentence: "He did not have much time." See Samuel Dubois Cook, "Is Martin Luther King, Jr., Irrelevant?" *New South* 26 (Spring 1971): 2.

CHAPTER FIVE

Conquer the Fear of Death
Advice for Living and Dying Well

King knew it would happen—death always does, and it happens to everyone. "There is an amazing democracy about death," he said. "It is not an aristocracy for some of the people, but a democracy for all of the people."[1] Knowing that it would strike him, too, King chose to face death with a double attitude. On the one hand, he fought it off, seeking to hold onto the life he loved, and on the other hand, he surrendered himself to its inevitability, facing it with deep trust in a God who is able to overcome the

---

[1]Martin Luther King Jr., *The Autobiography of Martin Luther King, Jr.,* ed. Clayborne Carson (New York: Warner Books, 1998), 232. The circumstances surrounding King's death are still in dispute. While some King scholars believe that James Earl Ray acted alone, others have come to believe that Ray acted with others, and even that the U.S. government should be implicated in his death. For example, Vincent Harding, "Martin Luther King and the Future of America," *Cross Currents* 46, no. 3 (Fall 1996), 312, has argued that "there is a very strong likelihood that the agencies of our federal government were deeply involved in his assassination." For a new study that offers a similar perspective, see William F. Pepper, *An Act of State: The Execution of Martin Luther King* (London: Verso Books, 2003); and Dexter Scott King, *Growing Up King: An Intimate Memoir* (New York: Warner Books, 2003), 273–90.

123

power of death. With this dialectical attitude, King believed that we can never do anything constructive in life—we can never live creatively, that is—until we begin to conquer the fear of death.

The Happiness of Not Sneezing

King did not want to die at all. Early in his public career, he offered a prayer that expressed the sentiments he held throughout his life: "Lord, I hope no one will have to die as a result of our struggle for freedom in Montgomery. Certainly I don't want to die. But if anyone has to die, let it be me."[2]

Unlike Christians who just cannot wait to arrive at the pearly gates, and so focus on heaven to the exclusion of earth, King said no to the death that awaited him. He fought death off because he felt passionate about his earthly life and all that it offered—the opportunity to lead the civil rights movement, the occasion to love, time to stop and chat with acquaintances as he walked to his favorite restaurant on Auburn Avenue, and even the chance to convert his vicious enemies. King simply loved this life too much to want to leave it behind.

His love of life, especially in relation to the inevitability of death, expressed itself virtually every time he recounted a letter he had received from a young girl shortly after his nearly fatal stabbing in New York City in 1958. The letter was prompted by a report in *The New York Times* that, given the blade's proximity to his aorta, King would have died had he sneezed while the blade was still in him. The young girl reacted to this news by telling King that she was *so* happy that he didn't sneeze.

King agreed. In his last public speech, which he gave on the night before he was assassinated in 1968, King noted that if he had sneezed, he would have missed all the student sit-ins and the freedom rides. He would have missed blacks straightening their backs in Albany and Birmingham. He would have missed the chance to tell America about his dream, to see the March to Selma, to join his suffering sisters and brothers in Memphis. "I'm so happy," he said, "that I didn't sneeze."

---

[2]King, *Autobiography*, 102.

King simply loved life too much to want to die. "Like anybody," he said in that last speech, "I would like to live a long life—longevity has its place." Ever aware of his approaching death, King felt that longevity would give him the chance to watch his children grow, to work for the beloved community, to lead souls to Christ. A long life would give him more time to love—to spread *agape*.

Life's Ultimate Tragedy

King said no to death because he deeply loved the life that God had granted him, but he also said no because he was deeply familiar with the raw pain of death—and he did not like it one bit. One of his earliest formative experiences was the death of his grandmother, Jennie Williams. By his own account, Mama Williams held a special place in her heart for young King, and when she died he was just devastated. Garrow reports that King was so crushed he took a leap from the second story of his home, albeit a rather unremarkable leap that resulted in no injuries.[3]

But the death of Mama Williams provided King with his first encounter with the pain of death, and at that moment the young King came to realize that, no matter what Christians may say about the glories of heaven, death hurts—a lot. It hurts because it snatches our grandmother from us. No longer can we hear her sing, or sit on her lap, or smell her Christmas cookies. The young King quickly learned that death can be devastating: It can make us want to jump out of a window.

King felt that same pain when preaching at the funeral for the little girls killed in the bombing of the Birmingham church. When he concluded his sermon by saying, "Good night, sweet princesses," the congregation could sense the pain of death well up within his own heart and soul. When he said, "Good night, those who symbolize a new day," they could sense that, like the hearts of the family members in front of him, King's own heart was broken in two.

Rather than downplaying the agony of death, King emphasized it. Preaching at Ebenezer in 1966, he stated: "And then there comes life's ultimate tragedy, that *something* that always makes for a broken

---

[3]David J. Garrow, *Bearing the Cross: Martin Luther King, Jr., and the Southern Christian Leadership Conference* (New York: Vintage Books, 1986), 35.

heart." For King, that is what death is—a tragedy that breaks hearts. "And no one," he said, "can lose a loved one, no one can lose a mother or father, sister, brother, a child, without ending up with a broken heart."[4] King was speaking from personal experience: He knew exactly how his heart felt when his grandmother had died and when the Birmingham girls were murdered, and he knew how it felt when thinking of the possibility of the deaths of his own family, as well as his own. In the face of death, his heart just ached.

Because he loved his own life so much, and because he experienced the pain of death, King never warmed to the reality of death. Death, for King, is but another example of the imperfection of life.

Conquer the Fear of Death

Though he understood death to be life's ultimate tragedy, King did not suggest that we should try to escape from it. Like Paul Tillich, the subject of his dissertation, King called for courage in the face of death—courage to be.

Death is simply a fact of life for us to confront head-on as we seek to live creatively. As he put it in the 1966 sermon noted above: "Don't try to escape when you come to that experience. Don't try to repress it." Don't become cynical or bitter about it. Good Friday, in King's thought, is simply a fact of life. So "take your grief and look at it, don't run from it. Say that this is my grief (*Yes, sir*) and I must bear it. (*Yes*) Look at it hard enough and say, 'How can I transform this liability into an asset?'"[5]

King did exactly that. Though he grew weary of the death threats on his life, and though he expressed concern about his own safety, he clearly tried not to run from death. *But if anyone has to die, let it be me.* It is not as if he could have run from it in any case. In addition to the constant death threats he faced, one of the lasting impressions of the 1958 stabbing was a scar at the point where the blade had entered his chest—a scar that King saw as a precious reminder of the threat of death. Andrew Young reports that King would sometimes say to

[4]Martin Luther King Jr., "Guidelines for a Constructive Church," *A Knock at Midnight: Inspiration from the Great Sermons of Reverend Martin Luther King, Jr.*, ed. Clayborne Carson and Peter Holloran (New York: Warner Books, 1998), 107–8.
[5]Ibid., 109.

his followers: "'Each morning as I brush my teeth and wash my face, I am reminded by the cross-shaped scar on my chest that each and any day could be my last day on this earth.' Then he'd smile and say we'd better make sure that what we were doing was worth dying for."[6]

In King's view, one of the greatest challenges of creative living is not only to face death head-on, but to do so without fear. King himself found it difficult not to fear the daily death threats that came his way, and his friends believe that the threats clearly took their toll on his emotional state. Still, he often claimed that he had moved beyond a paralyzing fear of the countless threats: "I have learned now to take them rather philosophically…One has to conquer the fear of death if he is going to do anything constructive in life and take a stand against evil."[7]

Creative living, for King, thus requires facing death with courage and strength, even while trying to withstand its inevitability. Without courage in the face of death, we will become weak and ridden with despair, unable to respond to the creative mandates of the beloved community.

King claimed to believe, in the deep recesses of his heart, that he truly did not fear anyone who threatened his life. Even on the day before his death, when death itself was just around the corner, he stood before the gathered throng of his followers and announced: "I'm not worried about anything; I'm not fearing any man. Mine eyes have seen the glory of the Lord."[8]

Indeed, in King's view, it was the Lord who had provided him with the courage to be in the face of death. Such courage first emerged shortly after his grandmother's death, when his parents sat down with him and spoke about personal immortality. "My parents attempted to explain it to me," he said, "and I was assured that somehow my grandmother still lived."[9] King was assured that the Lord would allow nothing, not even death, to stand between Mama

---

[6] Andrew Young, "Introduction: I've Been to the Mountaintop," Martin Luther King Jr., *A Call to Conscience: The Landmark Speeches of Dr. Martin Luther King, Jr.*, ed. Clayborne Carson and Kris Shepard (New York: Warner Books, 2001), 202.

[7] Quoted in Garrow, *Bearing the Cross*, 393.

[8] King, "I've Been to the Mountaintop," *Call*, 223.

[9] King, *Autobiography*, 7.

Williams and the love of God. No, the Lord would never leave her, and she would never leave the Lord. The adult King held onto this childhood experience and allowed it to deepen in significance when he bowed down at the kitchen table shortly after receiving yet another death threat during the Montgomery movement. The powerful kitchen experience, described in the first chapter, is what sustained him most during the very real moments of discouragement.

"Having to live under the threat of death every day," he said late in his life, "sometimes I feel discouraged."[10] During the Chicago campaign, when King felt especially down, he expressed his discouragement in the clearest of terms: "I am tired of the threat of death," he said. "I want to live. I don't want to be a martyr. And there are moments when I doubt if I'm going to make it through."[11]

But he did make it through, in large part because he continually returned to the kitchen experience, when he heard that voice within tell him to stand up and continue the fight. *And lo, I will be with you. Even until the end of the age.* In the kitchen that night, King received the courage he needed to face anything, even death, along with the assurance that, no matter what happened, his Lord would not desert him. Trusting in the abiding presence of his Lord, King sought to conquer the fear of death. And so King believed that we can finally conquer death, and thereby free ourselves to live creatively, by trusting that the Spirit of the Lord will never leave us, no, never alone, no, never alone.[12]

The Second Coming and Judgment Day

Because he put great trust in the *abiding* presence of the Spirit of Jesus, King consistently refused to emphasize the traditional belief that Jesus will come again, physically, to judge the living and the dead. As a student, King had argued that the traditional belief that Jesus physically resided in the heavens made no sense in a Copernican

---

[10]King, *Autobiography*, 354.

[11]Quoted in Garrow, *Bearing the Cross*, 512–13.

[12]For more on conquering fear in general, see Martin Luther King Jr., "Antidotes for Fear," *Strength to Love* (Philadelphia: Fortress Press, 1981), 115–26. In this sermon, King argues that we can conquer fear by bringing the reason for our fear to consciousness, by taking on the virtue of courage, by practicing love and embracing its power, and by trusting in faith that God will make a way out of no way.

understanding of the universe. In King's thought, the notion that there is a physical heaven at all is prescientific nonsense.

Moreover, King offered a deeply spiritual argument against the second coming: "The most precious thought in Christianity," he argued, "is that Jesus is our daily friend, that he never did leave us comfortless or alone, and that we may know his transforming communion every day of our lives."

For King, the second coming of Jesus, an event that would supposedly mark the beginning of the dramatic end of earthly time, is not an event in space and time at all. "Actually," he said, "we are celebrating the Second Advent every time we open our hearts to Jesus, every time we turn our backs to the low road and accept the high road, every time we say no to self that we may say yes to Jesus Christ, every time a man or women [*sic*] turns from ugliness to beauty and is able to forgive their enemies."[13]

The young King also refused to depict the end of the world as a period of judgment when we would literally stand before Jesus as he recounted all of our sins in great detail. As a seminarian, King had agreed with the belief that Christ is not really a judge at all. "The highest court of justice," King observed, "is in the heart of man…Rather than being the Judge, Christ is the light in which we pass judgment on ourselves."[14] Judgment day, in this sense, is any day we judge ourselves in light of the life of Christ.

As he grew older, though, King did begin to speak explicitly of a judgment day in which the Spirit of Jesus acted as judge. In 1967, just one year before he died, he preached: "Oh, there will be a day." And on that day Jesus will not ask us about all our awards, popularity, education, or material possessions. "On that day," King said, "the question will be, 'What did you do for others?'"

We might say that we studied hard, worked hard, and saved hard, but if we say that, we should beware, for Jesus will take issue: "'But I was hungry and ye fed me not. (*That's right.*) I was sick, and ye visited me not. I was naked, and ye clothed me not. I was in

[13]Martin Luther King Jr., "The Christian Pertinence of Eschatological Hope," *Called to Serve, January 1929-June 1951,* vol. 1 of *The Papers of Martin Luther King, Jr.,* ed. Clayborne Carson et al. (Berkeley: University of California Press, 1992), 269–70.

[14]King, "Six Talks in Outline," *Papers,* 1: 251.

prison, and you weren't concerned about me. *So get out of my face. What did you do for others?*"[15] That will be the question of questions: What did you do for others?

Though he clearly suggested that the Spirit of Jesus would turn people away at judgment day, King never depicted a literal hell full of the flames of divine wrath and administered by the devil, and he certainly did not use the fire of hell as a tool to scare his listeners away from a literal hell. If anything, his use of the image of judgment day was a metaphorical call to ensure that we live a good life right here and right now. *What did you do for others?* Yes, the Lord is judge—so act for others now.

Further, we must act so much for others that we would be willing to die for them. As King understood it, creative living requires that we commit ourselves to others, without reservation, as we march together toward the beloved community. If we refuse to die for others on the march toward the beloved community, our life isn't life at all: We are already dead, prematurely dead.

Get Our Hearts Right

For King, the best way we can prepare for judgment day is by believing in God and doing our best to follow the will of God by dreaming of the beloved community, working toward that dream, withdrawing to refuel, and working even harder to make the dream come alive. That is the will of God, and it is the best way to die. Indeed, it is far better to be murdered while following the will of God than to rest in the comfort of our homes while following cultural expectations. "Every now and then," King preached in 1966, "I'll have to agonize and suffer for the freedom of his children. (*Yes*) I even may have to die for it. But if that's necessary, I'd rather follow the guidelines of God (*Yes*) than to follow the guidelines of men. (*Yes*)"[16]

What matters most, though, is that our hearts are right as we strengthen personal character and fight for social justice on the journey toward the beloved community. King fully realized that when we are at the last of our days, we may discover that our dream

[15]King, "The Three Dimensions of a Complete Life," *Knock*, 131 (emphasis author's).

[16]King, "Guidelines for a Constructive Church," *Knock*, 111.

of being in the beloved community is unfulfilled, to say the least.[17] As we look back upon our own lives, too, we may see a series of sins that implicate us deeply. We may recall incidents we have caused that resulted in the deepening of the world's sin, and we may uncover mistakes, terrible mistakes, we have made along life's path.

Fear not. "In the final analysis," King stated, "God does not judge us by the separate incidents or the separate mistakes that we make, but by the total bent of our lives." God knows the depths of our weaknesses and frailties. "In the final analysis, what God requires is that your heart is right."[18] And so a fundamental calling of creative living is to search our hearts: What is motivating us? What do we intend? Whom are we serving? "If your heart isn't right," King said, "fix it up today; get God to fix it up."[19] Creative living requires that we surrender our lives to the God who can set us on the right path, the One who can make a way out of no way.

For King, we know we are on the right path if someone can say about us, "He may not have reached the highest height, he may not have realized all of his dreams, but he tried." If someone can say that we tried to be good, just, and honest, then we are on the right path. If someone can say that our hearts were in the right place as we worked for the beloved community, we are on the way.

This is what King wanted others to say about him at the time of his own death—that he tried to do the will of God, come what may. Do not mention all my awards, he said. "I'd like somebody to mention that Martin Luther King, Jr., tried to give his life serving others."[20] Say that he tried to love somebody, that he tried to be right on the issue of war, and that he tried to care for "the least of these." Do not call him a saint—call him a drum major for peace, justice, and righteousness.

It is enough, then, that our hearts are right as we work for peace, love, and justice, and it is enough only because God is sheer grace. Trusting in the abundant grace of God, King preached—just one

---

[17]I agree with Peter Ling's assessment of King's last days: "The political tide had never been entirely on King's side, and at the time of his death it was clearly running against both him and his dreams," in *Martin Luther King, Jr.* (New York: Routledge, 2002), 5.

[18]King, "Unfulfilled Dreams," *Knock*, 196.

[19]Ibid., 198–99.

[20]King, "The Drum Major Instinct," *Knock*, 185.

month before he died—that God would accept even the sinner who tried, the sinner whose heart was right:

> And I can hear a voice saying, crying out through the eternities, "I accept you. (*Preach it*) You are a recipient of my grace because it was in your heart. (*Yes*) And it is so well that it was within thine heart." (*Yes, sir*)
> I don't know this morning about you, but I can make a testimony. (*Yes, sir. That's my life*) You don't need to go out this morning saying that Martin Luther King is a saint. Oh, no. (*Yes*) I want you to know this morning that I'm a sinner like all of God's children. But I want to be a good man. (*Yes. Preach it.*) And I want to hear a voice saying to me one day, "I take you in and I bless you, because you try. (*Yes. Amen*) It is well (*Preach it*) that it was within thine heart."[21]

Saying Yes to Death: Entering the Indescribable City

We should thus not worry at the time of our death if our dreams have not come true, if our actions have not led us to the promised land, and if our time on the mountain has not given us enough fuel to finish the faithful work of God's people. Instead, if our hearts are right while we have worked for the beloved community, we should trust that the God of grace will lead us, as King put it in 1963, "down that mysterious road called death and at last to that indescribable city he has prepared for us."[22]

Though he never believed in a physical heaven or hell, King also never surrendered his belief in personal immortality—the belief that began to take root when his parents had assured him that his deceased grandmother still lived on with the Lord. "Our earthly life," King wrote in 1963, "is a prelude to a new awakening, and death is an open door that leads us into life eternal."[23]

---

[21]King, "Unfulfilled Dreams," *Knock*, 198. Compare the assessment of King offered by Samuel Dubois Cook: "The character of the man was as remarkable, significant, and fascinating as his ideas and leadership. He was an exceptionally good, civilized, and sensitive human being. His character, integrity, spiritual strength, and moral courage were of genuinely rare quality," in "Is Martin Luther King, Jr., Irrelevant?" *New South* 26 (Spring 1971): 4.

[22]King, "Shattered Dreams," *Strength*, 95.

[23]Ibid.

Throughout his life, King remained true to what he had stated in seminary: "The Christian sees reality in immortality because he sees reality in God."[24] Death is an open door to eternal life because of who God is: "God is a God that will conserve all values of the universe." We will live again exactly because we are of value to God.

King believed that it is the will of God not only to conserve all values but also to bring them to fulfillment. In King's view, God understands that human life in particular consists of values and capacities that require a life beyond here for their completion. "Would not this be a strangely irrational universe," he wrote in 1963, "if God did not ultimately join virtue and fulfillment, and an absurdly meaningless universe if death were a blind alley leading the human race into a state of nothingness?" The question was rhetorical. For King, God will ensure that nothing, not even death, can stand in the way of human fulfillment: "His creative power is not exhausted by this earthly life, nor his majestic love locked within the limited walls of time and space."[25]

When our time on earth comes to a close, then, God will sweep us into time after time so that our potential might be fulfilled. The fulfillment will not be physical; heaven is not a physical place, replete with pearly gates and streets paved with gold. "For us," King wrote as a student, "immortality will mean a spiritual existence."[26]

But we should rest assured that our spiritual existence in eternity will be greater in quality than our physical existence here. Speaking at the funeral for the little girls of Birmingham, King offered: "Death is not a period that ends the great sentence of life, but a comma that punctuates it to more lofty significance."[27] This lofty significance will include the experience of eternal rest—a point King stressed when he concluded his sermon by paraphrasing Shakespeare: "Good night, sweet princesses. Good night, those who symbolize a new day. (*Yes*) And may the flight of angels (*That's right*) take thee to thy eternal rest."[28]

[24]King, "The Christian Pertinence of Eschatological Hope," *Papers*, 1: 271.
[25]King, "Shattered Dreams," *Strength*, 95.
[26]King, "The Christian Pertinence of Eschatological Hope," *Papers*, 1: 272.
[27]King, "Church Bombing Eulogy," *Call*, 98.
[28]Ibid., 99.

King believed that in life eternal God will give us rest—rest from our broken hearts, our unfulfilled dreams, and our divided communities. We will experience eternal rest exactly because God will make us whole: God will complete our personalities, taking away all the divisions we've experienced; God will fulfill our faithful dreams, taking away all the obstructions that wore us down; God will awaken everything within us that was dulled and lulled into sleep during our earthly existence. And with our potential fulfilled, we will be able to rest—eternally.

In addition, our eternal rest will not happen in isolation. King believed that in life eternal God will bring us into the beloved community, the fulfillment of the divine will, where all the people of God enjoy peace, love, and justice, as God intends. Life eternal, then, is communal. King's grandmother is there, the little girls from Birmingham are there, and King himself is there. We will be, too, according to King. If we let God get our hearts right, if we let God help us to serve others, if we let God help us reflect the sacrificial love of Christ, the flight of angels will take us, too, to the place of our eternal rest—the love of God.

King never dared to explain how all this would happen; his theology of eternal life never took on serious theological constructions. For example, King never offered a developed theory of atonement, as some Christians like to do. Instead, he was content to announce that "God through Christ has taken the sting from death by freeing us from its dominion."[29] Explaining how exactly God did that in Christ was of no real interest to King, but hope in the *experience* of eternal life often found expression in his life.

Salvation on Earth

While we are here, though, the last thing we should do is to obsess on heaven. "It's all right to talk about heaven," King said. "I talk about it because I believe firmly in immortality. But you've got to talk about the earth. It's all right to talk about white robes over yonder, but I want a suit and shoes to wear down here."[30]

As one who preached the social gospel, King firmly believed that the dream of heaven serves us best not when we see it as a "pie

[29]King, "Shattered Dreams," *Strength*, 95.
[30]King, "Why Jesus Called a Man a Fool," *Knock*, 146.

in the sky" that we will eventually enjoy, but when we allow it to impinge on the time of our life here on earth. For King, then, we would do well to live out the dream of milk and honey by letting it guide us to work for food for everyone on earth; the dream of the New Jerusalem by letting it guide us to work toward a new Atlanta, a new New York, a new United States; and the dream of absolute morality by letting it guide us to take the best road possible in a world of chaos and destruction.[31]

With this advice, King held to a fluid notion of salvation. Yes, life eternal is a place of eternal rest, a final end point where God fulfills the divine will. But for King, salvation itself is a process: "Salvation," he preached shortly before he died, "isn't reaching the destination of absolute morality, but it's being in the process and on the right road." It's a matter of believing in God and trying our best to do the will of God, come what may.[32]

In this sense, salvation is nothing less than creative living at its finest—believing that the Spirit of Jesus will never leave us alone; saying yes and no to the past, present, and future; dreaming of the beloved community that God in Jesus intends for everyone; making that dream come alive; and retreating to the mountain for refreshment so that we can work even harder for the dream that remains, even to this day, unfulfilled. At last, then, if we choose to live creatively, not only will we live well—we will die well.

---

[31]Ibid., 147.
[32]King, "Unfulfilled Dreams," *Knock*, 196.